SAVED SEX:

CHASTITY—
BECAUSE YOU'RE WORTH IT

MOLLY KELLY

T0204677

Copyright © 1997 by The Center for Learning. Reprinted 1999.

The Center for Learning
P. O. Box 910
Villa Maria, PA 16155

ISBN 1-56077-516-5

Printed in the United States of America.

Library of Congress Cataloging-in-Publication Data
Kelly, Molly
    Saved sex: chastity—because you're worth it/Molly Kelly.
      p. cm.
    ISBN 1-56077-516-5 (Center for Learning: alk. paper).
    1. Chastity 2. Teenagers—Religious life. 3. Sexual ethics
    for teenagers. I. Title.
BV4647.C5K45   1997
241'.66—dc21

                                  97-7817
                                    CIP

DEDICATION

I would like to dedicate this book to my husband Jim, who is still a source of inspiration to me, and to my 8 children and 9 grandchildren who are my treasures.

CHAPTER 1

THE OPENING OF A NEW SEASON

One of my favorite stories, regardless of what time of year it is, is Dickens's *A Christmas Carol*. I mention that because when I was thinking about how I would start this book, the Ghost of Christmas Future came to mind. Do you remember what that Spirit did? He scared the kajeebies out of old Scrooge by giving him a peek into the future and showing him what was going to happen if he didn't change his ways. I thought to myself, what if that ghost appeared to me twenty some years ago and showed me my future, would I believe what I saw? Would I believe that Molly Kelly would be speaking to over a million teens on *chastity*? Would I believe that I would be speaking not only in the United States, but also in Canada, England, Wales, and Australia, as well as to 6000 priests in Rome, Italy? No way! After all, twenty some years ago, I *never* spoke in public. Way back then, my husband Jim was alive, and I was immersed in the changing, feeding, and nurturing of eight little children. In fact, I was known as the hot dog lady because I ran hot dog day at my children's school, and my life pretty much took place in one of three places—home, school, or in the car. But a Spirit did come to me and touch my life, and this Spirit wasn't a ghost or a Dickens character. This Spirit had credentials! This Spirit was a bona fide member of the Blessed Trinity—the Holy Spirit—and my life has never been the same! Over the years, the Holy Spirit has healed my past, filled my future with joy and excitement, and stayed with me every moment of the present. Now that's an awesome Spirit!

The reason I want to share a little of my life with you is because I am sure that some of you will see yourself in parts of my story. Some of you will say, as I did, "There's no way that I would get up in front of teens and talk about anything, much less sex! Spare me O Lord!" As a matter of fact, in my college yearbook, under my picture, it says, "A little shy, a little sly." Ah, but God works best with those who need a lot of work. All it took was a *yes* from me.

Let me go back to February 1, 1975, and mark that day as the day that changed my life forever. In baseball, the first game is called the season opener, and in my life that's what this day turned out to be—the opening of a new season. But first, I had to find a reason to even get up in the morning. On February 1, my husband Jim Kelly, a physician, a man in love with his God, a devoted father, and the love of my life, was killed in a sledding accident. Needless to say, I was devastated, and that word doesn't come close to describing my loss. As they pronounced Jim dead, I quietly pronounced that I didn't know how I could go on living. We were partners for life, and his was over. At that time, my oldest child was 12 years old, and my youngest was 14 months old. Let me back up and tell you a little about Jim, because Jim not only left me with eight children, he left me with his mission. I knew I would be the one to raise our children, but I didn't yet know that I was also the one that was to carry on his ministry. Oh, I'm not talking about my becoming a doctor, that was out of the question. First of all, I wouldn't have the time to go to medical school, and second of all, I had no desire to become a physician. Medicine to me meant Band-Aids and kisses, and anything else, I left up to Jim.

Jim was a radiologist, but if someone asked me today what kind of Doctor he was, I would tell them that he was a Catholic doctor! Jim believed with all of his heart that his hands were meant to heal and never to harm people, and that his Catholic faith was his code of ethics. On January 22, 1973, the Supreme Court, for the first time in our nation's history, legalized the killing of unborn children, and I suppose that I could say that that was Jim's season opener. Jim heard the news report, and because he believed that physicians were to be healers, not killers, from that day on, Jim spoke out in defense of life. Jim was a prophet. Pretty bold statement Moll! Yep, but it's true. He saw what would happen if he did not speak out, and so he spoke! Let me insert here that I honestly believe that many of us are called to be prophets (or prophetesses if you are gender conscious), but not enough of us audition for the role. Jim did, and his was no bit part. He helped found Pennsylvanians for Human Life, an organization dedicated to promoting a respect for all human life, and he became a spokesperson for **life**. In fact, on January 22, 1975, Jim was the keynote speaker at a memorial service commemorating the infamous *Roe v. Wade* decision. Ten days later, Jim was dead.

CHAPTER 2

1976 A.D. (AFTER DEATH . . . JIM'S)

I needed to share my Jim with you because it was through his death that my ministry took life. I became somewhat active in Pennsylvanians for Human Life, although I had very little time to do anything outside the home. My kids were into every-thing—sports, clubs, climbing trees, skinning knees, fighting, making up, doing homework, not doing homework—and my life was always trying to fit twenty-four hours of things to get done into a daily schedule where I knew they'd never get done!

As time passed, I missed Jim so much that I decided I wanted to try speaking on the abortion issue in high school classes. I felt that if I did what he did, then I would feel his presence in my life, and I did, and I do! But let me tell you, it didn't come easy. I had never spoken in public before Jim died, and I already shared with you what my college classmates thought of my oratory prowess. At first, I stammered and stumbled and lost my train of thought a lot, but then Moses was a stutterer, and look what he accom-plished! Actually, it's not ever what *I* accomplish, but rather what the Holy Spirit accomplishes through me, His weak and empty instrument.

I have to be honest, the Holy Spirit is somewhat of a newfound friend for me. I grew up praying to God, picturing Jesus, and the Holy Spirit was someone that just flew in and out for the occasion of my Confirmation and I hadn't seen hide nor wing of Him since. I began to become more and more aware of the Holy Spirit, so on a whim and a prayer, I decided to invite Him into my life . . . and **kaboom, wow, zowie** . . . let me tell you, it was the best thing I ever did! Oh, I still have to prepare my talks, practice them in front of the mirror, or in the dining room, or outside in the yard to the birds and squirrels, but the Holy Spirit is always there at delivery time when I get up to give my talk in front of a real live audience. That's not to say that everyone always agrees with everything I say, or even likes it, but I "speak the truth in love," and you know who appreciates that more than anyone else—teens! Teens hate hypocrisy! They want you to say it like it is.

Teens today are used to confusing double messages, and they find it refreshing and very affirming to hear someone challenge them to the moral highground. I once had a teen come up to me after a talk and say, "I don't agree with you but thanks for coming and speaking to us, your respect for our generation really shows."

Here's a little formula that I go by in my talks, and you are welcome to try it.

> I am not there to impose my morality, I'm there to expose immorality.
>
> I am not there to give a conflicting message, I'm there to give a convicting message.
>
> I am not there to confuse my listeners, I'm there to diffuse (spread around) the truth.
>
> And, I am not there to further desensitize people, I am there to resensitize them!

This formula works because it allows people to make a choice about their sexual behavior. The choice I offer is the best one—*chastity*. The choice then becomes whether to accept or reject the message. I explain that to students by saying, "Choice is good, but choose well, because choice is brief but unending." A principal at a public school gave me that line, and I use it all the time.

CHAPTER 3

FUEL!

Over the years, I've been asked a lot of questions regarding my ministry, but the two that seem to interest people the most are: "How do you keep going?" and "Where do you get your energy?" My answer to both is God! God is my fuel! If He was going to call me out of darkness (Jim's death, plus my never having spoken in public before Jim's death), then He was going to have to be my light, and He is—when I let Him! To be honest, the only time I feel overwhelmed is when I think that it all depends on me—when I forget that I am just along for the ride and that He is at the controls! As Mother Teresa says, "I am just a pencil in God's hand," and I can tell you that He is quite an artist, with different strokes for different folks, and each one is His masterpiece!

Some famous artists are known for their still-life paintings, but this master paints me moving, and from Him I draw my energy. God knows each of us, inside out and upside down. After all we are His creation, and He knows what each of us needs to keep going. On most trips, I usually speak at four school assemblies a day, and then again in the evening to parents. Each talk is anywhere from forty-five to sixty minutes, and I expend mounds of energy "chastityizing" my audience! Do you want to know how God fuels me? I am fueled through daily Mass, reception of the Eucharist, and through other people. The daily Mass and Eucharist part are pretty self-explanatory. You need food to live and to have energy, and you need spiritual food to live in Christ and to have the energy to "Do whatever He tells You"! Remember that neat story about the marriage feast at Cana? The newly married couple ran out of wine at their reception . . . pretty embarrassing . . . and Mary noticed their chagrin and told Jesus the problem. Jesus balked a little and even asked His mother what that had to do with Him, but Mary, having complete trust in the kindness and compassion of her Son, told the waiters to do whatever her Son told them, and we all know what happened. Jesus made wine out of water, and not only that, it was far better than the first batch! In fact, it's still the best wine ever made—vintage year 30 A.D.! It's never been matched! Why not let Him make us "Vintage Jesus," because that's what we become when we do whatever He tells us. God also fuels me through people, and I'll be sharing with you some of that "gas" as I go on.

CHAPTER 4

WHAT ABOUT CHASTITY?

So far, all that you know about me is that I am a mother and love being one, and that I am a speaker and am amazed at being one! I told you a little about my life and how my ministry really took shape and took off because of my husband's death. Actually, to be more precise, I'd have to say because of his life. I watched Jim agonize over the legalization of abortion, and how it deeply troubled and saddened him because babies were being killed by men and women in his profession. I watched Jim prepare a full-page statement for the *Philadelphia Inquirer*, a newspaper that purports to print all the news that's fit to print, but, like so many other newspapers, it prints only the news it sees fit to print, and only how it sees it!

In this statement that cost $4000, an amount that worried me but not Jim, he wrote that all human life was sacred from the moment of conception to the moment of death, and that abortion was the destruction of innocent unborn life and was against all moral, medical, and ethical standards. The money was to be raised by the physicians who would agree to sign this statement. Jim sent out letters to members of his profession, and 300 physicians sent back a "yes" and a check. This statement appeared in the Philadelphia newspaper one year before the Supreme Court of this nation chose to condemn to death all those precious little wombdwellers who fell into the category of unwanted or unplanned.

This statement made somewhat of a stir, but the legalization of abortion had not yet happened so to some it was a piece of science fiction. After all, this was the land of the free and the home of the brave! This was a country that proudly proclaims liberty and justice for all. Those doctors must come from outer space to write such a far-fetched statement! Well, the next year it did happen! The Supreme Court legalized abortion and, in doing so, made the words "liberty and justice for all," a sham, a shame, and a lie! Jim didn't gloat with an "I told you so" attitude. Instead, he simply vowed to make it his life's work to try and right this terrible wrong. Jim was "the doctor of La Mancha"! He dreamed the impossible dream and tried to right the unbearable wrong, and I inherited from him his passion to protect life (and my love for windmills).

I told you all of this as a background to how I got into the chastity message. To some, abortion and chastity may seem to have nothing to do with each other. But to me, abortion is the problem, and chastity is the solution. There are so many abortions because of so many unwanted pregnancies because of *sex!* There's the connection, and that's how I became known as "the chastity lady"! If life is sacred, then so is how that life begins. By God's design it begins with the sexual act, therefore the sexual act is sacred. It is kind of like that logic course I took in college that taught that if A=B and B=C, then A=C!

CHAPTER 5

CHASTITY MY FOOT!

I have been begged, beseeched, and implored to use a word other than chastity. I hear, "C'mon Moll, get real. 'Chastity' sounds like a biblical word, and it isn't going to fly!" Others have told me that the term chastity is archaic and out of date. The truth is that because the word *chastity* had not been used that much in the past twenty years, teens don't come into an assembly with a preconceived aversion to it. Hey, they rarely if ever have even heard of the word, and that works in my favor because I can then introduce them to the concept of chastity, making it a positive challenge rather than a negative scolding.

When I decided I wanted to write a book about chastity, I considered naming it *Chastity My Foot*. That title, which the publisher talked me out of, seemed to capsulize the reaction many people have when I tell them that I talk to teens about chastity. If I told them that I talked about abstinence, there would still be those scoffers and unbelievers, but not as many. So why don't I use the word abstinence if it seems to go over better with more people? My answer is that abstinence is not what I talk about! Abstinence is a negative word with a negative connotation, and it gives off negative vibes, especially to teens. I am very careful not to make anyone think that I perceive sexuality as something bad. Abstinence is a great word to use in drug education because using drugs to get high is bad. The same goes for alcohol education. Teens should not drink alcohol. They should abstain until they reach the legal age to drink, and then only drink in moderation if they choose to drink. There has been a tremendous effort in recent years to get young people to abstain from smoking because it has been proven that tobacco is harmful to our health. Every cigarette package states that right on it.

My point is that the word abstain is often used with things that are harmful. I do not want to put sex in that category. Our sexuality is a beautiful God-given gift, and it was meant to be enjoyed, treasured, respected, and protected. By the way, at the beginning of every school assembly, I tell teens that everyone of them has sex! That remark is usually received with looks of "I don't believe she said that!" Some of the teens, in fact many of them, shake their heads *no* to my bold claim, and the whole assembly becomes really quiet. Of course I have to explain my remark, so I ask them if any of them have ever filled out a form. Many of them nod yes. I tell them that most forms ask for the name, address, and sex of the person. After they fill out the name and address part, I ask them what they put after the word sex. Do they put "Yes," "No," "Sometimes," "Good," "Excellent," or, simply "male" or "female"? I point out how society has taken the noun *sex* and made it a verb, and, in doing so, society has blown it way out of proportion. The word *sex* on the form is simply asking our gender. Are you male or female?

I think that it's important to define some words before I go any further. *Sex* is our gender. *Sexuality* is our personhood, who we are, and how we relate to others. *Sexual intercourse* is the bodily union of man and woman by a sacred act that scripture describes as the two becoming one. Everyone has sex! Everyone has sexuality! But not everyone has sexual intercourse, nor should they if they are living according to God's directions! God ordained that sexual intercourse belongs in marriage, where the man and woman can pledge to each other fidelity, faithfulness, and foreverness! Whenever sexual intercourse is taken out of marriage, it is wrong and sinful. Tough words but true words.

It is so difficult for our young people today because they are the first generation to be taught by some people in authority—teachers, parents, counselors, and even some clergy—how to engage in sexual intercourse and "not get caught," meaning not get pregnant or contract a sexually transmitted disease. This is not to say that all adults have caved in on our young people, but far too many have, and the results have been devastating. There are almost one million pregnant teens each year.[1] More than a quarter of a million teens abort their babies each year.[2] Three million teens contract sexually transmitted diseases each year, and the number of HIV infected teens is absolutely frightening.[3] The Center for Disease Control recently reported that AIDS is the number one killer of young adults between the ages of 25 and 44. This indicates, because of the AIDS incubation period, that there must be a huge number of HIV infected teens.

What I really find upsetting is that those who report statistics are rarely apt to include the emotional and spiritual consequences of promiscuity. Many teens are experiencing feelings of fear, frustration, loneliness, anger, rejection, heartbreak, and despair, and there's no contraceptive that can fix those hurts or make them go away. I tell teens that there is no condom big enough to fit over their heart and their soul. And what about the spiritual fallout? Sex outside of marriage is a sin, and sin carries with it feelings of guilt, remorse, sadness, and despair for those who do not know of God's forgiveness. I am high on teens. I believe that they are a great generation and that they deserve 100 percent foolproof protection against the harmful side effects of sin! I offer them a surefire solution which I call *saved sex*, and I debunk, as poppycock and a big fat lie, the concept of "safe sex" as the solution to anything. Our young people, as well as everyone else in the world (I always think big!) are worth the first and best answer and nothing less! Didn't God offer us that on the cross? God sent His only Son to die for us that we might have eternal life, and that should give us an idea of our inestimable worth in God's eyes!

[1] The Alan Guttmacher Institute, *Facts in Brief: Teen Sex and Pregnancy* (New York: The Alan Guttmacher Instsitute, 1996).
[2] *Ibid.*
[3] *Ibid.*

CHAPTER 6

SEXUALITY—GIFT OR BURDEN?

Our good and awesome God who made each of us to His image and likeness never intended for our sexuality to be anything but a gift. It is only in our misuse of the gift that the gift becomes a burden. God never said, "Here is your sexuality, but it's evil, bad, and dirty. Be ashamed of it. It only gets good if you get married!" He also didn't say, "Here's your sexuality, but you're going to have to use pills, condoms, drugs, and devices to control it." No way! Our God said, "Here's your sexuality. Enjoy it. Treasure it. Respect it. Protect it." And then, being the good God that He is, He gave us the gift with a clear set of instructions, a warranty, and a maintenance agreement!

Think about it. Most gifts come with directions that explain how to use and take care of the gift. Let's say that the gift is a hair dryer that someone gave you for your birthday. The directions tell you how to use it and where to use it, or better yet, where not to use it! For instance, an electric hair dryer is never to be used in the shower, if one is to avoid "shocking" results! The hair dryer also comes with a warranty direct from the manufacturer, guaranteeing that if it is used properly, then the manufacturer will stand behind its product, reimbursing the consumer if the product fails. But the warranty applies *only* if you use the product according to the directions given by the manufacturer! When I buy a large appliance, I always pay extra for a maintenance agreement, which means that if the product fails or breaks during the term of agreement, then it will be fixed free of charge, or I will receive a new appliance.

What does this have to do with our sexuality? Everything! God has given us the gift of sexuality, with a clear set of directions found in the Ten Commandments and in Scripture. This gift of sexuality is wrapped in and backed by God's word! God has told us to flee fornication, which is premarital sex, and to avoid adultery, which is extramarital sex. I believe that sex outside of marriage is a lie and that it means taking something that is not ours. Therefore, the Commandments telling us not to lie or steal also apply to our sexuality. God's word is filled with directives and counsel on how to use the gift of sexuality according to His design. I strongly recommend a daily dose of God's word. A passage a day keeps the devil away! And that's the truth!

Let's take a look at the warranty on our sexuality. If we use the gift of sexuality as God designed it to be used and enjoyed, then it can help us be happy, healthy, holy people. If we misuse the gift of sexuality by going against God's directions, then it can lead to disease, destruction, despair, and even death. The reason that AIDS is now the number one killer among young adults is not because God poxed us with a plague, but it is rather because of the misuse of His gift of sexuality, and the misuse of drugs.

I bet that you're wondering how I'm going to tie in the maintenance agreement part! Our God is an all-forgiving God, and because He knew that we would be weak and sinful people, He sent His only Son to die an excruciatingly painful death on the cross, so that sins would be forgiven. We are called by God to respect the gift of sexuality, our own as well as that of everyone else. When we fall prey to the workings of satan, which is called temptation, then we must tell God that we are sorry, confess our sins, and promise that we will try not to commit those sins again.

I like to call God's forgiveness "White Out"! Anyone who has ever written a term paper knows what "White Out" is. When I was a little girl, we used ink eradicator, a chemical that smelled so bad it scared the misspelled words off the page! The fragrance of God's forgiveness scares our sins right off our souls and leaves us smelling like roses! Why is it that so many Christians carry so much baggage around with them when it is so unnecessary. I travel a lot, and I pack very little. In fact, when people pick me up at the airport, they automatically head for the baggage section, and I tell them that I have everything with me. I pack light because it saves my shoulders and my neck! The more I bring with me, the more I have to carry, and the more I carry, the more my shoulders ache. Conversely, the more we sin, the more baggage we carry with us, and the more we carry, the more we hurt. Why not give it all to God because His shoulders are stronger than ours. Didn't they hold the cross that saved us all?

God is the God of everyone, and His forgiveness is for everyone who asks for it with a humble and contrite heart. I am a Catholic, and I believe that the Sacrament of Reconciliation is a tremendous gift that so many of our young Catholic teens are not opening. What good is an unopened gift? Think about it. People pay a fortune to go to psychiatrists and, for some people, such treatment is necessary. But if more of us would go to confession, confess our sins to Jesus through His priests, and be truly sorry for having offended Him while promising to try and not offend Him again, we would be healthier people. Make no mistake about it, holiness is a healthy lifestyle, and it doesn't cost one cent! It's already paid for in full by our Savior, and at what a tremendous cost to Him—His very life!

Whatever religion you might be, or might not be, God's forgiveness is for you, and I would urge you to ask for it, accept it, and be grateful for it!

CHAPTER 7

YES!

I use the word chastity because it is a *yes* word rather than a *no* word. I already explained how abstinence has a negative ring to it. Furthermore, abstinence just deals with the sexual act, and that single focus opens up the concept of abstinence to different interpretations. There are those people who have actually taught teens that abstinence only has to do with saying no to the act of sexual intercourse. In other words, everything and anything else they do with and to each other is okay, as long as they stop in time. That's like driving on a superhighway at 65 miles an hour and seeing a red light. Oh, you'll be able to stop, but not in time. You'll pass the red light, and you will crash and get hurt if something is in your path. I tell teens that if they don't want to arrive at the destination, then they should not keep driving in the same direction! Foreplay is reserved for marriage because it is meant to lead to sexual intercourse. It's part of the process.

That's the beauty of the word chastity. It deals with the whole person, rather than just the sexual act. Chastity means sexual self-control. It means understanding our sexuality and how God intended for us to enjoy it. Chastity means refraining from sexual intercourse before marriage, and it means having sexual intercourse in marriage. A married couple, sharing that sacred sexual act with each other and only with each other as husband and wife, is practicing chastity. But chastity includes a lot more than that. A chaste person dresses modestly. Now there's a word that we need to dust off and put back into people's mouths, minds, and hearts. Let me tell you what modesty does not mean. It doesn't mean covering ourselves from head to toe, with no skin showing! It does have to do with the way we dress, however. I like to put it this way—the more you show, the more difficult it is to say *no*. The more that's revealed, the less the mystery! There used to be an old song (much older than I am, but my grandparents sang it!) called "Ah Sweet Mystery of Love," and the point of it was that true love would get better each day because there would always be new things to learn about each other, new places to go, and new things to talk about. I'll talk more about modesty later in the book.

Chastity also has to deal with what people are willing to put in their minds via books, television shows, movies, magazines, and music, and what they allow to come out of their mouths. A chaste person never uses vulgar language that demeans sexuality, and a chaste person does not watch actors and actresses lusting after each other and bedding down with anybody and everybody because sex sells movies. "R" rated films are a dime a dozen, and they're not even worth that! I tell young people that the "R" stands for raunchy! In order to earn the "R," the film has to have explicit sex, explicit language, or explicit violence, and if it has all three, it stands for *rich* in Hollywood's mind!

There was an article in the *Wall Street Journal* about a study done by a research team. It seems that retail advertisers hired this team to find out what it is that would make teenage girls want to buy their product—because teenage girls represent a huge amount of purchasing power each year. The results were intriguing and insulting. This team boldly declared that the advertisers must put sex in their ads because that's what appeals to teenage girls. Sex brings in big bucks, and that's what Hollywood, Wall Street, and the music industry are after! How do we fight back? We need to expose those that are manipulating teens for the money mongers they are.

Young people love music. It's their second language! In fact, most of us love music. Me, I like the mellow stuff, the golden oldies, the radio stations that have *easy* after their call numbers. I like to be able to decipher the lyrics. When my kids were younger, I could always tell when they borrowed my car. I'd turn the motor on and be blasted out of my seat by loud, screeching, unmelodic sounds! Perhaps it was their generosity that made them want to share their choice of tunes with whomever was within a ten mile radius! My kids get hysterical when I sing the songs from my day. *Shaboom Shaboom* was not what you call sexually arousing!

Today's music is a lot different. Some of the music is great, but the lyrics to some songs are inappropriate. Singing about having sex, wanting sex, and dreaming of sex has an effect on teens. It desensitizes them. Sex becomes *no big deal*! Sex is a big deal because each one of us is a big deal, and if you ever doubt your worth, take yourself in front of the crucifix! Make sure that it's a crucifix with Christ on it. Empty, smooth, shiny crosses won't work in this exercise. Spend some time just looking at His bloody, battered, dead body hanging by nails on that cross, and that will help you realize how much you are worth. Because of Him, you and I are *priceless*!

CHAPTER 8

CHASTITY ACCORDING TO JAY LENO

One night I was lying in bed, with the T.V. on, a book on my tummy, and, as usual, I was fast asleep. I watch T.V. for the weather, news and sports . . . nothing else! I always fall asleep in the middle of the news, before the weather and sports segments begin! Luckily, my kids always come into my room to tell me that they are home and to say goodnight. They turn the T.V. off, put the book on the shelf (always losing my page), and turn off the light. What goes around, comes around! That's what I did for them all those years, and now they are tucking their Mommy in bed!

This particular evening I was in "ZZZsville," as my kids would say, when I was startled by the phone ringing. I jumped out of bed on the first ring, and answered, "What's wrong!" My kids call me Spaz. They tell people that their Mom used to have them dead if they were home five minutes late! That might seem ridiculous to some, but for me it works. They know how much I worry so they always call and tell me if they're going to be late. I'm not as hard on my married children. I don't make them check in with me, but I still check in with them. Spazzes don't change easily!

As I held the phone with my trembling hand, I heard my son Patrick say, "Mom, you were on 'The Tonight Show with Jay Leno!'" I assured him that it must be someone who looks like me because I was in bed. But Pat persisted, "Mom, Jay Leno just talked about you!" Now my Patrick is somewhat of a tease so I told him that I thought it was a little late to be playing some practical joke. Patrick replied, "Jay Leno talked about you and chastity on his program." Now this really piqued my interest. Chastity discussed on "The Tonight Show"? That had to be a first! Part of the Leno line-up is to take newspaper articles and use them as fodder for his jokes, and on this particular show I was his fodder. I had just given a talk in a public school in Massachusetts, and a reporter was there to cover the story. Jay held up the newspaper article and said, "Wait until you hear this. Molly Kelly, mother of eight, is in the area giving talks on chastity!" Then he laughed and looked right into the camera and said, "Physician heal thyself!"

The next morning I took up my pen and wrote Jay Leno. I told him that I didn't mind being made fun of. What I did mind was that he was making fun of chastity, and it was obvious that he had no idea what it meant. I then proceeded to give Jay Leno a chastity talk! I explained to him that the word chastity does apply to married people, that Jim and I had eight children while practicing chastity, and that chastity and children do go together. Jim and I were faithful to each other, and we only shared that special gift of sexual intercourse with each other as husband and wife in a chaste relationship. I'll bet you're dying to hear what he wrote back. He didn't! That didn't matter to me, because just writing the letter made me feel better. I also determined that someone on his staff must have read it and, therefore, someone on his staff now knows the meaning of chastity!

Speaking of T.V. shows, let's take a look at an ordinary day of television viewing. There are talk shows galore, with sad, sad people discussing abnormal and often immoral situations. Husbands talk about their affairs with other women and why they do it. Wives talk about being beaten by their spouses and why they let them do it. Mothers talk about falling in love with their daughters' boyfriends. Girls talk about sex; boys talk about sex; Dr. Ruth talks about sex; advertisements talk about sex; and if you think I'm making it up, turn on the "boob tube," or "plug in drug" as my friend calls it, and see for yourself.

I was asked to be on one of Oprah Winfrey's shows a few years ago. I was told that the subject was going to be abstinence and that I would be the advocate for abstinence—the chastity cheerleader! The date of the show conflicted with another speaking engagement that I had already committed to, so I declined the invitation, although that decision was not as easy as I make it sound. I know that the listening audience of Oprah's show numbers in the millions, and the program director was doing his best to get me to cancel the other engagement and come to Chicago for the show. He couldn't believe that I would even consider turning down a chance to reach millions with the abstinence message. I had to let him know my answer within two hours. I talked to some of my friends as well as to my kids and asked their opinion. Everybody was saying "Go for it!" I called the woman who was my contact person for the talk I had already agreed to, and asked if I could get out of it. She was disappointed but told me that it was up to me, and she would understand and accept my decision. I took myself away from everyone and decided to ask God what he wanted me to do, and it didn't take very long for His answer. It was very clear to me that God isn't impressed with national T.V. exposure, and that I was to speak in this little town in New York to the people I had already said "yes" to! What I did do was to put the program director in touch with Leslee Unruh, another national chastity speaker and a delightful person. Leslee did the show. She called me later and said it was a real setup. The topic wasn't abstinence. It was about teenagers having sex at home. The debate focused on parents who actually allow it and who tell teens to put a necktie on the doorknob of the bedroom so that no one will walk in on them!

In all fairness, Oprah does seem to care about teens, but this show was a free-for-all, with Leslee holding her own but coming away very discouraged. She told me that the good that came out of it was that she became an instant "celebrity" and was getting calls from everywhere to congratulate her and to ask her to come and speak. It just proves that God always triumphs, but we have to let Him be our program director!

CHAPTER 9

THE GOOD OLD DAYS!

Some people have accused me of wanting to go back in time, to what they refer to as the good old days. Oh, I have fond memories of my childhood because I was blessed with a good family, but I wouldn't want to go back for the world. I like today! I think teens today are more sensitive and caring than in my time, and since my ministry is primarily to teens, I love what I'm doing!

I do have to say that I think life is more difficult for teens today. To repeat for the umpteenth time, and I'll say it some more before you finish reading this book, the messages young people hear today regarding their sexuality are conflicting, confusing, and desensitizing. That was just not the way it was during my teenage years. Actually, the subject of sex wasn't even talked about much, but the message was as clear as could be. It was implicitly understood that sexual intercourse belonged in marriage and we were not to engage in it or in anything that led to it. We knew this without having teachers in school show us explicit pictures of sexual organs or teach us about pills, condoms, spermicides, diaphragms, IUDs, Norplant, etc., etc., etc.!!!

And, guess what? There wasn't a teen pregnancy problem when I was a teen. There wasn't an epidemic of sexually transmitted diseases. Oh, there were some, but very few. Today there are over fifty strains of sexually transmitted diseases, with chlamydia and HPV being the most virulent among teens. Now I like learning new words, but chlamydia and human papillomavirus aren't words that I'm excited to learn. Abortion wasn't even discussed in my teenage years. Abortion was considered a terrible wrong, and people who performed abortions were considered "sleazebags." In my day AIDS was a good word. It referred to people that helped you. So, now you might ask why I don't want to go back to those "good old" days. To repeat, I like today, and I like the teens of today! I believe that the answer isn't in going back, but rather in exposing the bad things about today and changing them.

This is the first generation that has been told a whopper of a lie! "Safe sex" is a relatively new term, coined for this generation. I looked up the word "safe" in my dictionary, and here is what it said: free from harm; involving no risk. How can anyone call any contraceptive pill or device "safe" knowing that it can fail—often does fail—and that when it fails the consequence can be *death*! That's not my definition of safe! Some people now use the term "safer sex" to cover the failures. My question to them would be, "Safer than what?" I learned in English grammar class that if you put an "er" on an adjective, it makes it better—rich, rich*er*. I'd rather be richer than rich, so it sounds to me like safer is better than safe! Perhaps it could be called "kind of safe" or "sort of safe" to be more honest.

The term "safe sex" means to use something, eat something, wear something, or insert something in or on your body if you're going to have sex. We are told only the median failure rate of each method. Most studies give the condom a 10 to 17 percent failure rate. In addition, a study in the 1996 summer edition of *Family Planning Perspectives* magazine reports that "The proportion of abortion patients whose pregnancy is attributable to condom failure has increased from 15% to 32%." This magazine is a publication of the Alan Guttmacher Institute, the leading proponents of birth control for teens!

I fly a lot, and I don't like to fly because I never understood how that huge, heavy piece of metal stays up in the air. I can tell you right now that if an airline told me that their planes get there 68 percent of the time, I'd avoid that airline! When I was on my way home from Australia, where I had the privilege of speaking to over 13,000 teens in seventeen cities, I noticed a sign on the ladies' room door in the Melbourne airport. It said, "Travel safe, pack a condom." I said to myself, "Is that what keeps those planes up?" Another time, I was in front of an audience of parents, and I asked the question, "Can you get AIDS from not using a condom?" I said to them that if they thought they could, to raise their hands! You would not believe the number of people who raised their hands! I looked at them and said, "Don't you have to do something else?" They all quickly put their hands down and said, "you have to have sex!"

In the vast majority of cases, AIDS has to do with *behavior*, thus the solution to AIDS will also have to do with behavior! If it is the sexual behavior that causes the problem, then condom use will not make it go away.

The condom industry is a crock! No other industry in the world would be allowed to get away with what the condom industry gets away with! It is allowed to sell a product as a protection to a deadly disease, call it "safe" knowing that it often fails, and, if it fails, they are not held liable because the consumer was told that the product may fail. Did you know that the condom package has an expiration date on it? Did you know that the condom is supposed to be kept in a cool, dry place? How about those trucks that transport the condoms across the country? Are they refrigerated? Did you know that the condom is no protection whatsoever against HPV? Did you know that the HIV virus is fifty times smaller than standard latex holes in condoms?[1] Think about shooting a BB through a volleyball net. That's about what the hole in the condom looks like to the AIDS virus! Did you know that the birth control pill is no protection at all against STDs and AIDS? The Department of Health and Human Services publishes a brochure warning that the condom does not eliminate the risk of contracting AIDS, it only reduces the risk.

I don't know about you, but this "safe sex" stuff sounds mighty risky to me! If we used all of the money, time, talent, and energy that is spent pushing condoms and pills to push chastity, the world and everyone in it would be better off!

I'd like to share with you what one young man said to me after he heard me speak to the student body in his high school in Orlando, Florida. He came up to me and told me that he liked my talk. In fact, he had a big smile on his face. He told me that

[1] C.M. Roland, ed., Rubber Chemistry Land Technology, reprinted in *The Washington Times* (April 22, 1992).

he was sitting next to a buddy of his who kept whispering to him during my talk, "When do you think she is going to drop the bomb?" His friend asked him this every ten minutes. Finally, when he realized that the assembly was almost over, he said to his friend, "I don't think she's going to drop the bomb!" I had no idea what he meant, so I asked him, "What does dropping the bomb mean?" He said, "You didn't offer us condoms at the end!" In other words, he was expecting me to add the condom message to my talk. He had heard other speakers talk about abstinence, but no one ever used the word chastity. And other speakers would talk about abstinence but would throw in condoms for those who were going to have sex anyway.

Today's generation of young people are confused because they are receiving mixed messages. One of my reasons for writing this book is to urge everyone who reads it to realize that our young people are worth the chastity challenge and very capable of living it! But, keep in mind that we can't *give* the message unless we *live* the message!

CHAPTER 10

VERBAL ENGINEERING

Someone other than myself made up the term *verbal engineering*. I can tell you who said it to me, but I don't know if anyone said it to him, so suffice it to say, I'm borrowing it! I first heard it used in this context: "All social engineering is preceded by verbal engineering," and isn't that the reason that abortion and promiscuity have been accepted as legitimate choices by so many in our society today? If you call the killing of babies a "right" and a "choice," it sounds American! If the phrase "abortion destroys a child" is changed to "abortion terminates a pregnancy," it is easier to swallow. If the term "safe sex" is used for giving young people the tools to do the very thing that causes the problems we want them to avoid, it sounds smart. It is all in the way something is said.

I talked about the so-called "good old days" in the last chapter. Now let's explore the evolution of certain words, and see how they have drastically changed over the past thirty years. Because I want you to see these words, side by side, I'll make a list, give you the generally-accepted meaning of these words when I was a teenager, and give the too-often-accepted meaning of these same words today. My point is to bolster my claim that it is very difficult for young people today to understand right from wrong. Making harmful and sinful behavior seem acceptable, because it sounds acceptable, is a dirty trick! Before I go any further, I do want to say that the vast majority of teachers and principals that I meet, in Catholic, public, and Christian schools, are there because they care very deeply about young people. It is almost impossible to remain in education if you don't like your students. I write this book not to condemn other adults but rather to point out that teens are not the only ones who have been hoodwinked by this verbal engineering. Many adults have also fallen for it.

Here is the list of words:

My Teen Years	Present-Day Teens
Safe—Free from harm; involving no risk; good, warm, comfortable, protected	**Safe**—Wearing a seatbelt; using a condom; taking a pill; having a legal abortion
Sex—Gender—male or female; a sacred act reserved for marriage	**Sex**—"Doing it," "making love," "sleeping with"; a normal activity that's part of growing up
Sexually responsible—Relying on self control; saying *no* to sex outside of marriage	**Sexually responsible**—Relying on birth control; saying yes to sex whenever you feel like it, but using "protection"
Condoms—A contraceptive device sold under-the-counter at the local drugstore (ineffective in preventing life)	**Condoms**—A contraceptive "wonder" sold everywhere and even distributed in some schools; promoted as a solution to AIDS; (ineffective in preventing death!)
Pill—A drug given to sick people to make them well	**Pill**—A birth control drug given to well people to prevent pregnancy (often making them sick)
Abortion—An abominable act that kills a child in the womb; wrong in all circumstances and against the law	**Abortion**—Termination of a pregnancy; legal and a woman's right (and against God's law)
Choice—One of many options; an American privilege; freedom to do what you should	**Choice**—Name given to the Pro-abortion movement; freedom to do what you want

I love watching the television coverage of the Olympics and am always astonished at what the gymnasts can do with their bodies! Likewise, I am astonished at what these verbal gymnasts can do with words. They can turn them upside down, inside out, give them a new spin, and come up with an entirely new meaning in the process! If you ever watch gymnasts getting ready to perform, you will notice them doing a lot of stretching. Verbal gymnasts do stretching too, but with the meanings of words. Every four years, young people from many different nations gather in the host country to participate in the Olympic games, and the world watches as they run, jump, swim, dive, or catapult their bodies into the air in somersaults and twists that defy gravity. Why is it that society accepts the fact that young people can be trained and disciplined to do such impossible feats with their bodies, but when it comes to moral discipline and training for today's youth, some people ignore it or call it impossible. The big NO-NO at the Olympics is drugs. Any athlete who tests positive for illegal drug use is banished from the games. Yet we have thousands of young girls who are put on the "pill" because some adults don't believe that they have the moral discipline to control their bodies! The "pill" is a drug! Make sense to you??

Young people are growing up with new translations of old words and, for some of them, the result has been an acceptance of dangerous and immoral behavior.

I believe in progress, but redefining words to make evil sound good and good sound dumb and out of date is not forward thinking. It's downright backward and backhanded! Let's take a look at some words that were meant to apply to every age. The Ten Commandments are what I call "Golden Oldies," and neither the words nor their meanings should be tampered with, "modernized," or changed, because such tinkering greatly displeases the AUTHOR! And speaking of love let me look at two more words before I conclude this chapter. *Love* and *dating* are words that are often put together and frequently in the wrong order! Doesn't *dating* and *love* make more sense? After all, we have to know people before we can love them. When I was in grade school, I learned that God made us to know Him, to love Him, and to serve Him. Notice the order of those words. First comes *know*, then comes *love*, and then comes *serve*. We can't love or serve a God we don't know.

Dating provides the opportunity for two people of the opposite sex to get to know each other by sharing ideas, values, dreams, hopes, and—if the chemistry is right—to fall in love. Ah, but in today's mixed up world, the word *love* has been spindled, mutilated, and bent so out of context that for some it's unattainable and unexplainable! The terms "making love" and "love makes the world go 'round" make love sound like it belongs in a factory or planetarium. How about "love at first sight"? Doesn't that phrase make love and infatuation synonyms when they are really antonyms—opposites! Infatuation is based solely on feelings. It can be fleeting and it makes no demands. Love is rooted in knowledge. It has a strong, forever flavor and love demands respect.

Next, we're told that "love is as soft as an easy chair," but sometimes it can be as hard as a wooden bench! Why? Love involves discipline, and discipline can cause discomfort. If I were going to buy an easy chair, I'd go to the furniture store and plop myself down on a whole bunch of chairs and "test seat" them, buying the one that felt the best to me. But love, although it can and should feel good, can't be bought, and it never involves trying people out or using them for one's own pleasure. Dating can be a happy and fun experience, or it can be an occasion of sin. It all comes down to respect—the major ingredient of love! St. Paul said it best when he told us that love is patient, kind, never rude, and never jealous. Those are great dating guidelines.

Here are a few other guidelines to help make dating a happy, healthy, and holy experience.

- Establish boundary lines and make necking, petting, and prolonged kissing "off limits"!

- Avoid occasions of sin. Teens should say no to unchaperoned parties, drugs, and alcohol. Individuals old enough to drink should be extremely careful because alcohol affects everyone, regardless of age.

- Don't go off to dark, isolated places. Know your date so that you will know what kind of behavior to expect.

- Don't tempt, tease, or titillate your date. It's not fair, and it's not smart!

- It takes *two* to say yes and only *one* to say no!

- Don't give mixed messages. Say no with your voice, your body, and your clothes!

- Take God along with you on your date. He's there anyway! If you have any doubt as to the morality of what you are about to do, just ask God! God will speak to you through your conscience, and if you feel uncomfortable about your actions, that's God's way of saying stop! Dating, love, and God! Now there's a great trio, and if you and your date always make room for God, then the three of you will have a great time together! The same goes for married couples. Marriage is also a threesome. Praying together as a couple is the glue that makes marriages stick together. If you both love, honor, and obey God, then loving each other will be a breeze!

CHAPTER 11

MORE CONDOMANIA!

At the risk of some people thinking that this book is becoming "overcondomized," I'm going to spend a little more time putting holes in the "safe sex" argument. A few years ago, Magic Johnson, a superstar on the basketball court, revealed to the world that he had the HIV virus. He called a press conference to announce it, and the media was there three deep! This was big news, and it was bad news. How could someone so famous come down with a virus about which we know so little? How did he get it?

Magic Johnson told the world that he became infected by having sex with a woman who had AIDS. Now, it's pretty obvious that Magic didn't know that she was infected with the AIDS virus or he would never have taken the chance. But, what if he did know? What if she said to him, "Magic, I have something to tell you. I have AIDS." Do you honestly think that he would have said, "I have nothing to worry about. I'm using a condom!" There's an old saying that goes like this "What you don't know can't hurt you." In this case, however, what you don't know can kill you!

AIDS is scary, not only because it kills, but also because it deceives! A teen sees Magic Johnson with the HIV virus, looking healthy, appearing on TV, making money, and the teen might say, "HIV doesn't look that bad to me." I'm sure that all of us wish Magic Johnson the best, and, better than that, let's pray for him. Magic is a carrier of the HIV virus, for life, and if it turns into full-blown AIDS, it will cost him his life. Most people who die from AIDS are alone at the end, or with only a very few of their family and friends who are privy to the tragic sight of a body covered with sores and ravaged by pain. Some AIDS patients live five, ten, twelve years before succumbing, and they look pretty good until the last year . . . when no one sees them.

It's important for us to know this and to tell young people who sometimes think that they are invincible. I tell teens that some people live ten years with AIDS, and if they think that's a long time I remind them that that will put most of them somewhere in their twenties. That seems to bring it home. Some have older brothers and sisters in their twenties, and that really makes the whole thing real to them.

As I have already stated, I speak at school assemblies, at the junior and senior high level, and I am always excited and delighted at the positive response of students to the chastity message. I speak in public, Christian, Catholic, and private schools, and although I may have to modify the wording of my talk to fit the school, I *never* modify the meaning. My message to all students, regardless of their religious affiliation or non-affiliation is *chastity*!

I once spoke to teens in a detention center. Most of them were there on drug-related charges. I was asked to come and give them a talk on chastity because this detention center saw a correlation between drugs and sex. Kids on drugs are often into sex and have a history of pregnancies, abortions, STDs, and sexual abuse. I entered this little room where six teens were sitting. I smiled at them, introduced myself, and proceeded to talk about the gift of sexuality and how we can start over at anything. I so much wanted to build their self-esteem and self-worth. I wanted them to know that I came because I thought that they were worth this message. They showed no emotion and barely looked at me as I spoke. They didn't make fun of it, but they weren't having fun listening. I worked even harder to tell them that once they left this place they had a whole life ahead of them and it could be a good life if they worked at it. I was emotionally drained after the talk, feeling that it went nowhere and that I was a bust! As I walked out, one of the teens, a young girl, followed me out and asked me if she could have my autograph. That was her way of saying "thank you."

Another time I was asked if I would speak at a school for the mentally handicapped. The counselor who invited me did so because she was very upset at the curriculum that she was given to teach her students. Because these kids were mentally handicapped, the curriculum stressed the need for pills and condoms because it wouldn't be good "if these kids got pregnant." The implication was that these kids might have kids like themselves and that would cost society money. I'll never forget the day I spoke there. There were about twenty-five students, ages twelve to twenty I surmised. Most of them were Down's Syndrome children. One boy ran around the room for the entire duration of my talk, and the teacher just smiled and nodded for me to go on and not to worry. The teachers there were extremely fond of their students and it showed. I prayed on the way there, asking God to put in my mouth what He wanted me to say, and how He wanted me to say it. I talked about the gift of sexuality, and how God made us all different but all of us to His image and likeness. I talked to them about chastity, what it meant, and explained the term saved sex. I ended by reminding them that sex is so good it's worth waiting for . . . and marriage is where it belongs. I then told them that they were so good that they were worth waiting for. After the talk a young girl with Down's Syndrome came up to me all excited. She had a big smile on her face. She looked at me and said, "I'm worth waiting for," and believe me, that made my entire ministry worth it!

When I speak at a public school I have to delete the God part (the best part!). This bothers me, but I must do it because we live in a nation that has so grossly misinterpreted the separation of church and state concept, turning freedom *of* religion into freedom *from* religion. I do not separate myself from God when I talk. I tell God that He has His work cut out for Him, and that although I can't say His name, I ask Him to speak through me . . . loud and clear. On one particular day when I was driving to a public school in Maryland, I said to God, "Because I can't say your name, doesn't mean you can't come with me today! God, please jump out of me and let the students know you are there." I gave my talk to about eight hundred kids, and, as soon as I was finished, a young girl came up to me and said, "Are you a

Christian?" I smiled and said to her "You bet!" and then I quietly said to God, "Thanks!"

After speaking in schools for over fifteen years, I now have a treasury of wonderful stories. They were the catalyst for writing this book. I wanted to share with you how wonderful our young people are. They hear the chastity message, they digest it, and for most of them it seems to go down pretty well. I didn't want to say they swallow it because that sounds like it was forced on them. I never force the message, I offer it to them and tell them that I do so because they deserve to hear it!

One time when I was speaking in a school in California, a young man came up to me after my talk, shuffled his feet back and forth, waited for everyone else to leave the room, and then looked at me and said, "I'm a virgin and you made me feel proud." Now you might say, "If he was so proud, why didn't he say it in front of everyone?" I would answer, "Thank God that he listened to me and felt good enough about himself to come up and tell me that he was a virgin."

Speaking of California, I spoke in a public school where there had been a recent controversy. The principal told me that he had been vilified by the press for sending home two girls who came to school dressed as condoms. It was Halloween time, and the students were allowed to come in costume. The principal told the girls that their condom costumes were inappropriate and that they had to go home. The parents of the girls came to the school and complained, but the principal held his ground. The parents didn't stop there. They went to the school board and to the press to explain that their daughters were being responsible in coming as condoms. After all, condoms save lives so their daughters were lifesavers. It makes you wonder, doesn't it? These parents have traded their common sense for condom sense which makes no sense at all!

Our young people will hear mixed messages at some schools, but if they also hear them at home, that's a double whammy! **No parent has to give a mixed message, and no parent should give a mixed message!** Whose kids are they anyway? Do we *send* our children to school, or do we *give* our children to the school? If more parents realized that schools must answer to parents for what they are teaching, then all schools could be teaching the saved sex message instead of the "safe sex" lie! So many parents homeschool because they do not like what is being taught in sex education. Not all parents can homeschool, or take their children out of the public school, so what we need to do is to take the offensive sex education out of school. Every parent should ask to see the curriculum on sexuality and read it cover to cover. If parents wouldn't say those things to their own children, why let the schools say it?

So often the sex ed course turns out to be sex training . . . teaching kids how to "do it" (have sex) and not "get caught" (get pregnant or catch a disease). Every sex ed curriculum should have a parent component so that parents are fully aware of what is being taught to their children. If parents do not like what is being taught, they should have the right to complain and, if that doesn't work, to take their children out of the class. At home, parents can add the God ingredient and talk about values and virtues. I also have to insert here that it is my firm belief that if one woman by the name of Madelyn Murray O'Hare can take God out of schools for the entire nation, then a few of us good Christian parents can put God back into schools! Impossible? Madelyn didn't think so, and she certainly didn't have God on her side. We do, so let's get started! **Now is the time for all good parents to come to the aid of their children!**

CHAPTER 12

TRY THIS ON FOR SIZE!

The following dialogues are fictitious. They highlight, through simplifying the conversations, the folly of some adults who give teens a double or negative message.

Father talking to his teenage son

> **Father:** Son, I don't want you having sex. It's not meant to be a casual or recreational experience. It has to do with commitment. Here's a condom.

> **Son:** Why Dad? What for?

> **Father:** To use when you have sex!

> **Son:** But you just told me not to have sex!

> **Father:** Yes, but you don't always take my advice, so I have to make sure I offer you another option.

> **Son:** Dad, do condoms always work? I mean, can I really have sex and not worry about getting AIDS, STDs, or some girl pregnant?

> **Father:** Well son, nothing's perfect. Condoms reduce the risks, but sometimes they fail. Let's hope they don't fail for you!

> **Son:** But Dad, what if they do fail?

> **Father:** We'll cross that bridge when we come to it.

> **Son:** Dad, don't you think it would be better if I waited until marriage?

Health teacher to class of teens

Teacher: Today we will be taking an in-depth look at "safe sex," talking about all the different kinds of contraception, how they work, how to get them, and how to use them. By the time this class is over, hopefully you will all be better contraceptors!

Student: Can we ask questions?

Teacher: Certainly. Now let's get started. Boys, you make sure you have a condom with you at all times. You never know when those hormones will act up. Always handle the condom extremely carefully, as the AIDS virus can pass through a pinhole! Also, remember to always check the expiration date, and the type of condom. I highly recommend the latex ones.

Girls, get on the pill. Talk to your mothers about it, but if they are being unreasonable, go to your local Family Planning clinic. You do not need your parents' permission, and they don't even have to know that you're on the pill. Of course, I'd be careful to always put them in an out-of-the-way place. Moms do snoop. Also girls, there is now something even better than the pill. It's called the shot! You simply get three shots over a three month period, and that will make you infertile for a certain amount of time. Check with the doctor as to how long. This will save you the worry of remembering to take the pill. I know that some of you forget to bring your lunch to school, so remembering to take a pill might be hard. Oh, and if you want to really be worry free, you can have a contraceptive implanted into your arm, and you won't even have to think about it for five years!

Student: Will we be looking at chastity as an option?

Teacher: Yes, I'll mention it, but it really doesn't work!

Student: Why not?

Teacher: Because AIDS is out there, and most of your generation wouldn't be capable of saying *no* to sex.

Students (in unison): Who told you that?

Teacher: All of the adult experts who study teens.

Mother talking to her teenage daughter

Mom: I don't want you to ever mess around with drugs! You are too precious to me, and drugs will hurt you. By the way, are you taking your birth control pill every day?

Daughter: Yes Mom, but I read the insert that comes with the pill, and it says that the pill is a powerful drug! It listed the most common harmful side effects, and they took up a whole page! Mom, I also read that hundreds of women each year die from complications of the pill!

Mom: Are you having sex?

Daughter: Mom, you put me on the pill which told me it's okay to have sex, so yes I am.

Mom: It isn't a matter of being okay. It's a matter of protection because it's not okay for you to get pregnant!

Daughter: Mom, I'm not enjoying having sex. It's a constant worry! Is he going to stay with me? Am I going to get pregnant? Did I take the pill? Will the pill work? Will it hurt me?

Mom: Well, if you do get pregnant, we can take care of it.

Daughter: How?

Mom: Abortion!

Daughter: You mean that if the pill doesn't work, I should kill my baby?

Mom: Those are harsh words!

Daughter: That's a harsh solution Mom, and I don't like it. I'm just not going to have sex until I get married and then I won't have to worry so much.

Mom: You always were a rebel!

Does all of the above sound a little negative and a little science fictionish? Well, sadly this is what's happening in some homes, and in some classrooms. Teens are being sold short, and some don't even know it! Ten years ago, distributing condoms in schools would have sounded outlandish! I'm from Philadelphia, and nine of our public schools make condoms available at school! It's time for us to act! Let's work to take condoms out of schools and put chastity in!

CHAPTER 13

LOOK INTO MY CRYSTAL BALL!

No, I don't believe in fortune tellers, ouija boards, palm readers, tea leaves, or anything else that pretends to tell the future! I can't tell the future, but all of us can look into the future and think about what's going to happen. Jim Kelly did that when he spoke out against abortion even before it was legalized. Dreamers do that. Visionaries do that. In fact, all of us look into the future to some degree. We work hard to make a better future for ourselves and for our families. In this chapter I'm going to ask you to look into the distant future with me.

The time is the year 2100. The place is the United States of America. The setting is a classroom in a public school. The assignment is to research the 1990s and do an in-depth study of the people "way back then." Find out what the social justice issues of the day were and what the people did about them. The student doing this assignment is your great-great-grandchild, and he or she has been told to find out what his or her ancestors—you—did about the injustices of the day!

I'm sure that by 2100, students will be able to go to a special room in the library, punch in the 1990s on a huge computer, and sit back and watch as this present decade unfolds in living color. What will the students think as a newsreel comes on showing the senseless slaughter of innocent people, on trains, in fast-food restaurants, and in office buildings? Won't they ask, "Why were they so violent? Why was violence so glorified in their culture?"

Next, the AIDS statistics appear on the screen and the student remarks, "Wow, those people had one major plague to contend with, and it wiped out half of the population before they realized that their behavior was the cause! Why did it take so long? Why were condoms offered as a solution when everyone knew that they couldn't stop such a deadly disease? Couldn't they see that the overwhelming majority of AIDS cases did not come from the lack of using condoms, but rather from sexual promiscuity and drug use? Why did so many people have to die before the chastity message and the "say no to drugs" message were the solutions offered to everyone, without exception?"

The screen changes and a sultry, sexy, semi-clad woman who went by the name of Madonna appears. The commentator remarks that she is one of the highest paid entertainers of the day. "Did people really pay money to see her do that?" asks the student. "Why?"

Sex, guns, killing, statistics on sexually transmitted diseases and AIDS, divorce, teen pregnancy—what will these students think of the 1990s? Won't they try to find out where we went wrong? After all, hindsight helps people do that! "Ah, there's the problem," says your great-great-grandson or granddaughter. "They permitted the slaughter of their offspring! They voted into office people who said that killing babies in the womb was a "right"! They had a Supreme Court that spent much of its time trying to protect the nation from God! Imagine! Young people in those days were not allowed to be taught about God! I'm sure glad that people came to their senses!"

By this time, the students of 2100 are getting depressed. They have come to the sad conclusion that the 1990s were no picnic! Now comes the part of the assignment that asks the student to find out what you, their ancestor, did to try and right the wrongs of the "raging '90s." Inquiries of relatives are made. Old newspapers are read, and your writings and personal effects are carefully studied. What will your great-great-grandchildren find out about you? Will they say, "I am really proud of my ancestor, and I am going to try to be like him or her"? Or, will they say, "I'm not sure if my ancestor did anything at all to try and stop the injustices of those days because I can't find any proof of it anywhere"?

The good news is that we still have time to change the course of history and work to fashion a brighter future—not to mention making our great-great-grandchildren proud of us! How? You can become a chastity spreader! You can work to put God back in schools. The first step is to make sure that God is in your home, in your family life, and in your heart. No one needs a crystal ball to be able to see disaster in the future if we don't do something to straighten out today. This world will never be a perfect place because perfection is reserved for His Kingdom, but we can make it a better place until His Kingdom comes! Check out the sex education curriculum in the schools in your area. Do it even if your kids have all grown up and are no longer in school. We need to care about all children. If the curriculum is "value free" and saturated with "safe sex" slop, do something about it! Go to the principal, whose salary you are helping to pay with your taxes, and make a case for chastity education. Go to the school board and do the same. Write an article for the local newspaper exposing the "safe sex" lie and promoting chastity—and don't forget to explain what chastity means. As old as that word is, and it dates back to before Moses, it's still unknown and misunderstood by so many. We need to reintroduce the term *chastity* into people's vocabularies. We need a chastity blitz! Maybe we could even get *The New York Times* to use it in one of its famous crossword puzzles: "What is an eight letter word that means living a pure, holy life?" How many people would write chastity as the response? The answer to that question lies with *you!* The more you spread the word, the more people will know the right answer!

CHAPTER 14

RECIPE FOR SUCCESS

Well, we looked back at the "good old days" and decided that as good as they were, they had their problems too. We just peeked into the future, and hopefully decided that we are still shaping it. So, let's concentrate on the present. In fact, I think that's what we should always do—live in the present in the presence of God! As a Catholic, the rosary is one of my favorite methods of prayer, and the Hail Mary is one of my favorite prayers. In the Hail Mary, we are told that the two most important times of our lives are **now** and at the **hour of our death**. If we live chaste lives now, then at the hour of our death we will be ready to meet the Lord, to be judged by the Lord, and to be welcomed home by the Lord. That sounds exciting to me. How about you? It certainly makes chastity an important ingredient to life. Let's take a look at the ingredients to chastity.

When baking a cake, *all* of the ingredients must be added for the cake to look right and to taste good. If you forget to add that dash of vanilla, extra egg, or baking soda, it could ruin the cake. Recipes only promise success if they are followed closely, and so it is with chastity! In the dictionary, the word *pure* is given as a synonym for chastity. If I asked you what kind of air you want to breathe, you would answer *pure* air. How about water? What kind of water do you want in our reservoirs? I'm sure that we all want our drinking water to be pure. As a matter of fact, we want pure ingredients in all of the food that we put into our mouths, and we rely on the Food and Drug Administration to make sure that happens. The reason we want *pure* water, air, and food is because we don't want any impurities *in* our bodies. Do we worry as much about impure actions *of* our bodies? Aren't they harmful too? Yes indeed! They make the soul sick, and that's why purity is one of the essential ingredients of chastity. If we add a healthy portion of purity to our lives, our lives will be healthy!

Another important ingredient of chastity is temperance. So many teen pregnancies are alcohol involved. Alcohol can make anyone vulnerable to poor moral decisions. Alcohol heightens the passions and deadens the conscience, and if temperance—moderation—is not practiced, then our sexual self-control could get out of control!

The other necessary ingredient to chastity is modesty. Modesty has to do with the way we dress. Let's face it, if we regard our sexuality as a gift—and we should because it comes from God—then shouldn't we gift wrap it? If you bought an expensive wedding gift for a friend, you certainly wouldn't just partially wrap it, or wrap it in cheap, dirty, unattractive paper. If you did, that would take away from the gift. The wrapping enhances the gift, and so it is with the way we dress. Our clothes can enhance or detract from the gift of our sexuality.

Today's fashion industry brings in big bucks, and immodest fashions are big sellers. Near nudity is commonplace in many Hollywood films, and low-cut gowns, thigh-cut skirts, and mighty tight pants seem to be the uniform for many female entertainers appearing on T.V. and in magazines. I know what you're thinking. She's picking on the girls! Doesn't modesty have to do with guys? It sure does, but it is my firm belief that women set the moral tone in society, and that modesty will become the "in" way to dress only if women set the standard. Ask the Wall Street experts who it is that buys most of the clothes, and they will tell you that it's women. Let's face it, women's clothes are more diverse than men's. Have you ever seen a low-cut tux? How about an immodest suit coat? Modesty in dress is just as important for men as it is for women, but I'm honing in on women because I'm a woman, and I'm a mother, and I believe that modesty must be taught and demanded by women! We are living in a culture that uses the female body in advertisements to sell everything from cars to cigarettes. The time has come for women to realize that they are being victimized!

Both male and female bodies are beautiful creations because they were designed by God, but, because of original sin, we can misuse our bodies by giving into temptations of the flesh. Adam and Eve didn't wear any clothes in the Garden of Eden, and that was okay way back then because God's original plan did not include original sin—nor clothes for that matter! But, we all know what happened. The snake tempted Eve, Eve tempted Adam, and all of us have been tempted ever since. Scripture tells us that as soon as Adam and Eve sinned, they realized that they were naked and covered themselves with fig leaves. In a way I suppose you can say that the fashion industry has Adam and Eve to thank for its booming business! It came about because of sin, and sin has colored much of it ever since! Now don't get me wrong. I like clothes, and I like to look nice, but, to me, a modest woman is more attractive and enticing than an immodest woman. There is a big difference between dressing to look sexually attractive and dressing to look sexually inviting. It goes back to that mystery thing I talked about earlier in the book. Sexual intercourse is reserved for married couples, and sexual intimacy should be their wedding gift to each other. The manner in which we dress affects those around us. If we wear clothes that seem to be inviting sexual intimacy, then we put ourselves and others at spiritual risk.

We all know the importance of having good role models in our lives, and for modesty, purity, and chastity, you can't beat the Blessed Mother! Mary is a virgin, pure, chaste, and undefiled, and we would do well to pray to her and ask her to help us act, dress, and live lives that are pleasing to her Son. No, I don't think that we have to wear long robes and mantles like Mary wore. They were the fashions of her day, and I'm sure that there were those who wore immodest clothes then too. Mary Magdalene probably wore immodest clothes during the prostitute period in her life, but, once she fell in love with Jesus, she dressed and lived for Him! When Mary the Mother of God appeared to the children at Fatima, Portugal, in 1917, she warned, "Fashions will much offend Our Lord. People who serve God should not follow the fashions." Mary further warned, "The sins which cause most souls to go to hell are the sins of the flesh." Mary's message must be heeded more than ever. Modesty invites chastity and chastity pleases God, so let me now give you some modesty guidelines.

M The *M*ore you show, the more difficult it is to say No!

O *O*verexposure can cause overheating!

D *D*ress your sexuality as a gift. Don't cheapen it!

E *E*xpress your sexuality. God gave it to you!

S *S*eductive clothes cause sinful acts!

T *T*asteful clothes temper temptation!

Y *Y*es to modesty means No to impurity!

This recipe for chastity—purity, temperance, and modesty—has been tested and proven, but you must add *all* three ingredients to make it chastity. Share this recipe with your friends and invite them to **taste and see the goodness of the Lord!**

CHAPTER 15

NOT IN TODAY'S WORLD

As you might guess, there are those who say that my (God's) message won't work. The three main criticisms seem to be as follows: "Your message is too old-fashioned." "You might win some over to chastity, but not all. Some people, and especially teen people, are going to 'do it' anyway." "What about those who have already had sex outside of marriage? The message doesn't even apply to them!"

I'll spend a chapter on each criticism because if you become a chastity spreader, and this **is** a recruitment book, then you will need to have answers for those chastity doubters. If someone has never heard the chastity message, the "safe sex" lie almost makes sense. After all, that's part of Satan's success story. Keep people in the dark about the word of God, and that will make them fertile ground in which Satan's lies can take root, grow, and spread. Since this nation has decided that young people in public schools should not hear the word of God, Satan's ploy is working. God uses truth to help us grow closer to Him. Satan's fertilizer is lies. Our public schools have many good things going for them, but they would be a lot better if God's word was allowed in the door!

Ah, there's the problem . . . whose God? Aren't there scads of different religions with different beliefs? What about atheists? Isn't it better not to offend anyone and just take God's word and prayer out of public schools? Hey, that offends me! My answer to such questions would be, "But why?" When the United States was founded, God was given top priority. The Declaration of Independence makes it clear that, "All men are created equal, and are endowed by their Creator with certain inalienable rights." The top three rights are life, liberty, and the pursuit of happiness. Today, both God and life have gotten the heave-ho! God has been expelled from the public school system, and life can be expelled from the womb by abortion. Our Pledge of Allegiance, written a long time ago, boldly declares that we are "one nation, under God." No one gave George or Abe a hard time about that! Our money still is inscribed with the words, "IN GOD WE TRUST." Our founding fathers didn't worry that such language would offend atheists. If we continue protecting our young people from God, then shouldn't our money have a disclaimer also inscribed on it—"For those who don't believe in God, this money is still valid tender."

If people do not know God's word, then their opinions and actions will be shaped by humans' words (whomever is teaching them and whatever is being taught). My point is not to criticize anyone who does not believe in God, but to point out that for those of us who know God's word, it is imperative that we share it with those who do not. Our gift is our burden. If I were a good singer (and I'm not too bad if the person next to me is on key), I would be asked to share my good voice at weddings, parties, and in church choirs. If I were a good cook, I'd be asked to share my recipes. I am a speaker, and my schedule is filled for the next year and a half. If God has given you certain talents then you will be asked by others to share them, and although it takes time and energy, the perks far outweigh the burden! It makes you feel good because you made others feel good! It is more important than ever before for people of faith to share the word of God with those who do not know it. That is the only way to turn our world around so that it gets better instead of worse. This includes spreading the chastity message. Chastity is a word of God, so let's start sharing it!

Back to the first criticism that I most often hear. "Molly, your message is too old-fashioned. It sounds like something out of the 1800s!" My answer to that criticism is that the chastity message *is* out of the 1800s, the 1700s, the 1600s, and it goes all the way back to the Stone Age, when that tablet was handed to Moses! Some people today point to the frightening statistics on AIDS, STDs, the illegitimate birth rate, abortion, and teen pregnancy and blame this upstart generation of young people. They'll say, "What's wrong with kids today?" Or, "Why can't they be like we were?" I look at those same statistics and blame the messages, not the teens of today. There is nothing wrong with teens today. In fact, I think that they are better than ever! I find them more sensitive, caring, and concerned than my generation of teens. Four of my eight children did a year of Catholic volunteer work after college. They gave a year of their lives to help others.

My daughter Mary Kate spent her year in a very poor section of Mexico. Mary Kate had majored in Spanish in college and wanted to go somewhere where she could speak that language. She worked at an orphanage, teaching and caring for the children. While she was in Mexico, Mary Kate fell in love! I used to get letters from her telling me all about this guy named David. She would write, "David is so cute." "I spent the whole day with David." "I hope you will get to meet David, Mom. I love him." Well, that did it! I decided that it was time for me to go down and visit Mary Kate, and check out this David fellow. I arrived at the airport, and Mary Kate said, "Mom, I can't wait for you to meet David." I replied, "Me too!" We drove to the orphanage and entered this empty room, at least I thought it was empty. Mary Kate said to me, "There's David," to which I replied, "Where's David?" Mary Kate said, "There, Mom." I looked down and there was David, a precious 20 month old hydrocephalic baby. Little David's head was swollen and filled with fluid. I looked at David and then looked at Mary Kate. Mary Kate wasn't looking at me, she was looking at David. She said to me, "Mom, isn't he beautiful!" I looked at Mary Kate's face and then back at David, and do you know what? The second time I looked at David, I no longer saw a little boy with a swollen head. I saw a beautiful child because I saw him through my daughter's eyes! That's what love can do! It has a beautifying effect! Instead of blaming young people for these horrible statistics, society better start looking at the bad messages it's giving today's young people. Let me say once again, the messages are confusing, conflicting, and desensitizing. Our young people are often told, "Don't have sex, but since some of you are going to anyway, don't do it without using protection. Hey, it doesn't always work, but what else can we do because you're going to have sex anyway." By making such statements, we create a self-fulfilling prophecy! If you tell a child that she is ugly, she thinks she's ugly, regardless of how pretty she really is. If you tell a young person that he is dumb, he thinks he's dumb, and that limits his potential to learn. If today's teens are told that they can't or don't have to say no to sex, as long as they are having "safe sex," then these teens will think that having sex is a rite of passage, and some will indeed have sex. As a result, those awful statistics will continue to rise as the moral standards continue to fall. I call the following outright declarations of hopelessness: "They can't say NO." "They won't say NO!" "We need to put condoms in the schools."

That's caving in on our kids, plus it's a CON job and it's DUMB! CONDOMizing and PILLaging people are negative non-solutions! The positive solution lies in CHASTITYizing them!

CHAPTER 16

THE "DO IT ANYWAY" BUNCH!

Criticism two can be answered in one sentence. **Chastity is a virtue for all seasons, all reasons, all people, and all times!** Chastity is inclusive not exclusive! It's for everyone!

Now let me get down to specifics. As far as the "do it anyway" bunch is concerned, living chastely, or not living chastely, is a matter of free will! God, in His absolute and unconditional love for us, gave us free will. In other words, we can do what He says or not do what He says, but there will be self-inflicted consequences for the "do nots." In Scripture, God is quoted as saying, "I set before you life and death, the blessing and the curse." Now, there's a choice! He also tells us what choice we should make if we truly want to be happy, healthy, and holy people. He tells us to "choose life." He doesn't make us choose life, nor does He force chastity on us, but He does make it clear to those who know His word that life and chastity are what we should choose. Some people might ask, "But why?" "If God made us sexual, then why is sex bad?" "How can sex be bad the day before you get married, then all of a sudden turn into something good?" "Should I practice chastity because I'll go to Hell if I don't?" In case you think that these are far fetched questions, I want you to know that I've been asked them all! These are fair questions and they deserve fair answers.

In my youth, oh so long ago, there was an answer that seemed to cover many of the questions we asked, and it was, "Because I said so." That was my father's stock answer, and it worked for us. I don't think that answer will fly today, nor do I think it should. There are good answers to these questions, and those of us who believe in young people, as well as in ourselves, should know them and give them.

As far as the answer of choosing life, we need only look at the alternative, which is death. We do not have to choose death, it will come. The question has more to do with the timing, thus the answer should have to do with God. After all, He gave us the gift of life. He made us. If a car manufacturer decides that there is something wrong with its product, the product is recalled. We are not products, but we are God's creation, and He will do the recalling when He feels it's time to perfect the gift!

As far as sex being bad, and only becoming good when one gets married, that's not God's reasoning. God gave us the gift of sexuality, and it is good. He ordained that that special part of the gift called sexual intercourse should be enjoyed only in marriage between a man and a woman who have made a lifelong commitment to each other. The purpose of the sexual act is unitive and procreative. It is the total giving of oneself to another in selfless love, and it is a willingness to allow God to create a new life by this sacred union. Contraception in marriage thwarts God's plan and limits love. Natural Family Planning (NFP) is in harmony with God's plan and teaches the couple to respect their combined fertility. NFP is a healthy lifestyle. It's inexpensive, drug-free, reliable, and it enhances love! I highly recommend NFP to married couples. For more information on Natural Family Planning call The Couple to Couple League in Cincinnati, Ohio, at 513-661-7612, or the NFP Center in Memphis, Tennessee, at 901-373-1285. They can refer you to classes in your area.

Outside of marriage, the sexual act is based on pleasure and selfish love—what feels good for me at this time of my life, and if I'm not ready for children, I'll use contraception and get my partner to do the same. That kind of love is rooted in pleasure, not commitment. It's often a fleeting love, trying out people as if they were products to be used and discarded at will. That's not God's will!

God respects us enough to give us the gift of free will, and respecting His will is the secret to using that gift properly.

I use the example of a fire to try and explain why sexual intercourse belongs in marriage. Sitting by the fireplace in front of a roaring fire on a cold winter evening is something most of us have experienced and enjoyed. In fact, it could even be called a romantic setting. A girl invites her boyfriend to come to her home and have dinner with her family. After dinner the young couple sits by the fire and listens to their favorite tunes. That makes for an enjoyable evening. What if there is no fireplace, so they decide to build a fire in the middle of the living room floor! You know what they have? They have about three minutes to get out of the living room because they just set the house on fire. A fire in a fireplace is warm, romantic, and makes you feel good. If you take the fire out of the fireplace and put it where it doesn't belong, then it becomes dangerous. Oh, it will still be warm, but it's out of control, and instead of making you feel good, it makes you feel scared. Sexual intercourse outside of marriage can still "feel good," but it's not where it belongs, and it becomes dangerous to our physical, emotional, and spiritual well-being . . . and that's scary!

I once had a girl ask me if she would go to Hell if she had sex outside of marriage. I didn't answer, "Yes, and if you have already done it, start packing." What I did do was to try and explain to her that God wants us to be happy, and that if we obey His command "to love one another as I have loved you," then we will realize that love involves discipline. Parents who love their children discipline them. They give them rules, limits, and guidelines to protect them from harm and to prepare them to meet the challenges of life. A little child is told not to cross the street by himself but to wait until his mommy or daddy takes his hand. Parents don't put ten snowsuits on a child in case the child runs in the street anyway, the theory being that if the child is well-padded, he or she won't get hurt! Doesn't that theory have a familiar ring to it?

I do believe in Hell, but it is not my place to say who is going there and who is not. That judgment is reserved for God and God alone. What we need to do is to teach people the truth so that they can avoid Hell! People choose Hell, they don't just end up there. God's mercy and forgiveness will always put us back on the road to Heaven, no matter how many times we stray or get lost. A mistake at work may cost a worker his or her job. An error in a test could spell failure. A misunderstanding between friends might end the friendship. But God's love is unconditional! If we commit a sin, are sincerely sorry that we have offended God, confess it, and promise to try our best to avoid offending Him again, then the sin is gone. God's mercy deodorizes the soul.

God never writes anybody off, and neither should we. For those who are going to "do it anyway," I'm still going to challenge them to the moral highground. I submit to you that most people, and especially young people, like challenges. How about if you and I were each holding the end of a stick a few inches above the ground, and we asked a five-year-old to jump over it. The five-year-old would not only jump over it, she or he would delight in meeting the challenge and immediately ask us to raise the stick. Offering the "safe sex" message is akin to lowering the stick! My guiding principle, no matter to whom I am speaking, is "What would Jesus do?" Would Jesus change the message for those who are going to have sex anyway? Picture Jesus hanging on the cross, looking out, and saying, "They're going to sin anyway, I'm getting off this cross!" He died for us precisely because He knew we were going to sin, yet He continually calls us to repent of our sins and to live according to His will.

Jesus never caved in on anyone! Sometimes people will ask me what I say to inner city kids, the assumption being that I would, or should, change the message for them. I may use different examples or stories, but the message remains intact! My talk doesn't put people in categories. As I said before, chastity is a virtue for all people, regardless of their ethnic background, place of residence, I.Q., or track record.

I'll never forget the time I received a call from a young man who asked me if he and a friend could come and meet with me. They had an idea for a group they wanted to start, and they wanted my input. These two young men are of African-American descent, and they told me that they were insulted that condom distribution was happening in the inner city schools. These teenagers felt that the predominantly African-American schools were being targeted on purpose. They felt that it was an assault on their character and an insult to their integrity to assume that because the illegitimate birth rate is high among African-American teens, that that proves they need condomizing! What it really proved to them was that the chastity message is needed more than ever. They told me that chastity was not being taught in the inner city schools, and that they would like to try and reach the kids themselves. I was so impressed with them. They formed an organization for teens called C.O.U.R.T. which stands for Chaste, Outstanding, Urban, Righteous Teens! C.O.U.R.T. is still in existence; it is growing; and it is taking the chastity message in rap form on the road. These young people are impressive emissaries of chastity, and they practice what they preach!

But back to the "do it anyway" bunch. The Say No to Drugs message is given in all schools, but it's a given that not all kids will listen, and that some will use drugs anyway. What about them? Should the school provide clean needles for the "do it anyway" bunch? All schools worry about teen drinking, and they have special programs around prom time to encourage teens to refrain from alcohol. Some kids are going to drink anyway. Should the school decide to have two proms—one for the drinkers, and one for the nondrinkers? The drinkers can drink, but they can't leave until they are sober. It's called "safe drinking." Or, should the school cancel the prom because some kids are going to drink regardless of what they are told. Isn't the answer for the school to establish rules, to tell students what kind of behavior is expected from them because the school believes in them, and to establish clearly the consequences if the rules are broken? Again, that's called discipline, and discipline is based on love.

Let me try out on you what some of our young people are hearing from some of out adults. "Don't take drugs. You can control yourself! Don't drink. You can control yourself! But, when it comes to sex, you can't control yourself! Here's a drug!" The birth control pill is a prescription drug. Do you want to hear how all of this translates to young people? "Don't use drugs, here's a drug! Control yourself, you can't control yourself!" Sound confusing? That's because it is! Think about it! If researchers found out that eating vegetables was the cause of the AIDS virus, what would we tell people? Would we tell them not to eat vegetables, to eat vegetables carefully, or would someone come up with a device called a Vegdom that would try and prevent most of the impurities from entering the bodies of those who are going to eat vegetables no matter what you tell them? Dumb example? No dumber than the con . . . dumb!

We can't scare people into practicing chastity. I believe that it is valid to talk about the consequences of living unchaste lives, but fear is the second best reason for chastity. **Love is the first best reason!** We must love others enough to want the best for them, and chastity is the best!

CHAPTER 17

THE "ALREADY DONE IT" BUNCH!

This is the most important chapter in the book! You're probably saying to yourself, "If it's so important, why did she wait until chapter 17 to write it?" I was building up for it! What this chapter proves is that chastity is for everyone—virgins, non-virgins, married people, clergy, homosexual persons, heterosexual persons, bisexual persons—everyone without exception!

Some people will say to me, "You speak at high school assemblies, and some of the students listening to you have already engaged in sexual intercourse." What about them? You don't expect them to listen, do you? My answer to them is, "Yes I do!" Because someone has already done something doesn't mean that that person has to keep doing it! When I am speaking to parents, I pose this question to them, "How many of you have taught your children not to lie?" All of them raise their hands and nod their heads in the affirmative. I then ask them, "How many of your children have lied?" Again they raise their hands telling me that they believe their children have told lies at some time in their lives. I then pose what I call a zinger—"How many of you, knowing that your children have already lied, now teach them how to lie and not get caught? Teach them to lie safely?" No hands go up! I then follow it up with this thought, "If your children are caught in a lie, isn't that the time you emphasize the importance of being truthful? Should we teach our young people how to steal, but make sure they have a getaway car, and call it "safe stealing"?

The "Say No to Drugs" message is given to all young people in all schools. It tells those who have never used drugs to continue to say *no*, and it tells those who are using them to stop! No one ever says to them, "Don't use drugs, but if you are already into them, have fun!" "Safe sex" says, "Let's teach kids how to have sex and maybe not get caught, with a baby or a disease being what they may catch." Why don't we just tell them to say *no*!

To drive home my point, I say to students, "Because I love excitement, how about if I decide to drive on the wrong side of the highway? It's more exciting! Everyone waves at me, horns start honking, and headlights start blinking. I know it's a little dangerous, but don't worry about me, I'm going to make sure that I have my seat belt on!" I tell the students that my seat belt might or might not save me from being killed, but there's no question that I will be wounded. My analogy is that while the condom may or may not protect those having sex outside of marriage from death—promising only risk reduction, not risk elimination—it will definitely not keep them from being wounded. We have emotions, and sex outside of marriage causes emotional wounds.

I opened up my home to five pregnant girls over the course of seven years, and I can tell you that it was the emotional damage that hurt them the most—the fear, rejection, anger, and heartbreak they felt. My children and I became extremely fond of these young women, and I was grateful to God that He put them in my life. These girls were good girls who made bad choices. They chose to engage in sexual intercourse outside of marriage, but they also had the courage and the moral integrity to choose life for their babies. So many women who choose to abort feel that they do not have any other option because no one has reached out to them and offered them the help they need to choose life. We cannot call ourselves pro-life, or Christian, if we are not there for those who need our help.

For every abortion facility that offers death, there should be ten crisis pregnancy centers offering life and the means to choose it. The good news is that there are over 4000 of these life centers throughout the United States. The bad news is that because they are not a business, they do not have the money to advertise, and, consequently, they are not as known as the businesses that provide abortion and birth control. Oh, the latter might call themselves non-profit but I have the right to call them otherwise because they are using taxpayers' money to promote their wares. A federal funding program called Title X contributes 140 million dollars to family planning centers, and contraception is their translation of family planning. Parents should be aware that Planned Parenthood and other family planning organizations are allowed to provide contraception to our teenage daughters without our knowledge or consent. In some states, teens are allowed to have abortions without parental consent. Every year, my kids would bring home a paper that had to be signed by me before they could start classes. Let me quote what it said: "The Pennsylvania Department of Health has issued new guidelines concerning the dispensing of medication in school. In order to dispense the following non-prescription drugs, we must have a signed permission slip from a parent or guardian. Please check the appropriate lines below, sign, and return to school. Your child will be given no medication without this signed form."

> _____ *Tylenol or Aspirin for headache or cramps*
> _____ *Gelusil tablet for an upset stomach*
> _____ *Robitussin DM for coughs*
> *Date* _____
> *Signature of Parent* _____

Think about it. Our teens need a signed permission slip to be given a non-prescription drug, but they can be given prescription birth control pills at family planning clinics without a parent even knowing about it, and it's funded by our tax money! Does that make you mad? Good! That's my intent! Couldn't you sue one of those ear piercing stands at the local mall if they put holes in your fourteen-year-old daughter's ear lobes, and you didn't want them there? If your daughter needs your permission to get her ears pierced, then why should she be allowed to undergo a medical procedure that kills your grandchild and wounds her, if you are living in one of the states that does not require your consent for her to have an abortion? Some states require parents to be notified if the daughter is going to have an abortion, but they can't stop her if she still wants it. Who wants the best for this girl—the government or her parents? Who will have to wipe away her tears and help her get her life back together—the government or her parents? Yes, some parents are derelict in their duties, but let's work to strengthen the family. Let's not give up on any parent or any child. Dream the impossible dream, and work and pray that it comes true.

The government has a program called Title XX in which less than ten million dollars is provided for the promotion of abstinence. Obviously, our government thinks that contraception is a better answer! I recently testified before a Senate appropriations committee to try and make a case for increasing the funding for Title XX so that more abstinence and chastity curriculum can be developed and made available in schools throughout the country. Pray that that will happen.

I call chastity *saved* sex. It applies to everyone. If some teens in my audience have already had sex then I challenge them to start saving again! After all, that's what you do with money. If you spend it, you start saving again, and guess what? It gains interest! I've already mentioned that those who promote "safe sex" call it the second best answer, to which I reply, "Since when were our kids worth the second best of anything, and can the word best be used with solutions that have known failure rates?"

I often ask students if their teachers accept the second best answer on a test. Would $2 + 2 = 5$ be close enough to be called correct? Any teacher who accepts an incorrect answer because it's the second best one is not a very good teacher, and I don't know of any who do that. When it comes to the question of sexuality, chastity is the first best and the only solution that's 100 percent effective, costs nothing, has no harmful side effects, and you can't get sick from it!

"Safe sex" takes our sexuality, which is a God-given gift, and by telling us that we will need pills and condoms to "protect" ourselves, it reduces our sexuality right down to the animal level. We are not the only species that reproduce, but we are the only species made to God's image and likeness, and we are given an intellect that enables us to make rational and moral decisions about the way we live as sexual beings. Animals mate and have offspring or litters. We mate and have children. Animals don't take vows or pledge fidelity and faithfulness to each other. We do. If a section of the country is being overrun by deer, one solution might be to extend the hunting season. If we don't want our pet dogs and cats to reproduce, we have them spayed, fixed, neutered or we keep them in if we know they are in heat. Imagine if we treated people like that! "John can't come out tonight because he's in heat!" "It's Mary's fertile time of the month, so we have to muzzle her." We are not animals! We are made to God's image and likeness!

When people tell me that the high statistics on teen pregnancy and teens with STDs confirm the "safe sex" solution, I ask them to point out the teens whom they are willing to concede, to give up on, to become a statistic. When studies show that the condom has a 10 percent failure rate in preventing pregnancy, does that mean that the person it failed for would only be 10 percent pregnant? If the child's genetic makeup is 100 percent complete at conception, and science has proven that it is, then the mother is 100 percent pregnant the moment she conceives. If the condom failure rate is 17 percent in preventing the AIDS virus, does that mean that the person it failed for would only get 17 percent of AIDS? AIDS destroys the immune system of an entire body. In fact, what if the condom only fails once, but you're the one it fails for, isn't that a 100 percent failure rate for you?

I'll give you an example that I use that points out the folly of statistics. My husband and I went away for the weekend to spend some time with friends and to do a little outdoor recreation. We decided to go sledding, and Jim, my husband, took the sled, went down the hill, hit an ice patch, veered off, hit a tree, and was killed. If you want to talk statistics, that was one in a million, but that was my one in a million! If someone came to me and told me that the number of sled deaths in 1975 was .000001 percent of all the deaths in the nation that year, I would tell them to jump over those 0s and get to the 1, and when they reached it, make sure they name it Jim Kelly, because he is part of that statistic.

Percentages and statistics don't matter when it comes down to moral decision making because there are individual lives at stake. Chastity is for everyone. I am there for the virgins, encouraging them to remain chaste. I tell them that there is no disease out there called "virginitis" and, in schools where I can say it, I hold up the blessed Virgin Mary as the best role model they could ever hope to emulate. For the young people in the audience who have already had sex, I invite them to start saving again. I use a gift analogy to get across my point, and it goes like this. What if a boy and a girl really like each other and they give each other a gift. She asks him to open his gift first. He opens it and takes out a necktie. He really likes it and tells her so, but then notices that the tie has some yellow spots on it. On closer obervation he realizes that they are egg stains and he asks her if the gift has been used. She tells him that she gave it to two other guys before him. He then asks her to open her gift. She opens it and sees a fancy lace handkerchief. She likes it at first, but when she lifts it out of the box she discovers that it is damp. She drops it and asks him if the hanky has been used before. He tells her yes, but only a few times. Both are disappointed in their gifts but decide to forget the gifts and go for a walk. He asks her if she would like a piece of gum. She says yes, and he takes a piece of gum out of his mouth and gives it to her. She tells him that she doesn't want his gum because he already chewed it! He tells her that there is some flavor still left in it!

A story like this one does not need any explanation. The young people immediately catch my drift! I end the story by saying, "The more you chew gum, the less the flavor. It's just something to chew! The more someone has sex outside of marriage, the less the meaning. It's just something to do." I tell them that sexual intercourse is a gift. Some gifts say "Do not open until Christmas" or "Do not open until your birthday." The gift of sexual intercourse says "Do not open until marriage," and I invite those who have already opened that gift prematurely to wrap it up again. That rewrapping of the gift is chastity for them.

If someone loses or gives away his or her virginity, that person cannot get it back. It's gone forever. In marriage, the gift of virginity is one of the greatest gifts a couple can give each other on their wedding night. If that gift has already been given away, then secondary virginity will rewrap the gift. Sometimes I call starting over "renewed virginity," "rekindled virginity," and even "recycled virginity" if it means to start saving again. Do young people believe that the gift can be rewrapped? Here is some living proof that they do.

I was speaking in Indiana at an assembly of about 1000 students, and I was pre-warned that I was going to have a rough time trying to convince them of my message. Some people don't like to be pre-warned because it makes them more nervous. Not me. I love it because it makes me call on God more than ever! In a situation like that I try to picture Jesus hanging on the crucifix, over the heads of all the students. I silently ask God to pour His blood on these young people that they might be open to the truth. Before every talk I also bind Satan by the name and power of Jesus. In other words, I tell him to go to Hell where he belongs and to leave me, and whomever I am speaking to, alone! Satan is one strong and powerful dude, but compared to Jesus, he's a wimp! I also call on the guardian angels of each person in the audience, plus my own, to provide a mantle of protection over the audience so that no evil spirit can enter and that only the Holy Spirit may penetrate. Hey, I'm no dummy. I know who I'm working for, and where to go for help when I need it, which is always!

This assembly was one of the best ones I have ever experienced. The kids were polite, receptive, excited, and gave me a rousing ovation! How about that for prayer power! After the assembly, a young girl came up to me and simply said, "Thanks for coming. I'm going to rewrap my gift." I felt like I had just hit the lottery!

At another school a girl came up to me and said, "I never realized that I could start over again. Thanks so much." This next story is straight from the mouth of an eighth grade girl, and it proves that when some young people hear the truth, they opt to live it. This young girl wrote me a letter after I spoke at her school. She thanked me for coming and told me that she really needed to hear the chastity message. She wrote, "A boy asked me to do it with him. I didn't know what to say to him so I told him that I'd think about it and tell him my answer on Saturday. You spoke at my school on Thursday, and after I heard you, I knew what to tell him. I told him that I was worth waiting for, and I was going to save myself for marriage." That's what I call super high octane fuel for my tank, or, 100 mile per hour wind for my wings!

I began this chapter by saying that chastity was for everyone, and that no one was excluded. I mentioned heterosexuals, homosexuals, bisexuals, virgins, non-virgins, married people, and anyone else you can think of. I do not want to categorize people, nor do I use terms to label anyone, but rather I invite everyone to practice chastity. For those who are homosexual, the chastity message does not condemn the person, but it does invite him or her to refrain from engaging in homosexual behavior. The homosexual inclination is not sinful, the behavior is. Being homosexual is rarely a chosen inclination, the problem comes in the act of homosexuality. There are many wonderful ministries to homosexuals that provide support groups, materials, and counselling therapy to help them live a chaste life. No one should judge or condemn others, but condoning immoral behavior can never be called love. When something seems too difficult or downright impossible, that's when we have to rely on God's grace. As Mother Teresa so eloquently states, "Nothing is impossible with God."

The following is an example of one such ministry:

Father John Harvey
COURAGE
c/o St. Michael's Rectory
424 W. 34th Street
New York, New York 10001

212-421-0426

CHAPTER 18

PEER PRESSURE: + OR -?

The title of this chapter looks like a mathematical equation! In math, the equation, if applied properly, can produce the correct answer. So can peer pressure, but the pressure applied must be a positive force, not a negative one. When my kids were just little tots, I used to get them to eat foods they were not crazy about (everything healthy!) by pretending the food-filled spoon was an airplane zooming in for a landing and their mouths were the landing field. If that tactic didn't work I would say, "Don't you eat this" . . . using my singsongy, "betcha can't" voice, and they would then open wide and eat even vegetables! Ah, but that didn't work when they got older. In fact, I had to tell them to forget that ploy or else I would have had my teenagers doing things that I told them not to do, but that they did anyway, because I clapped my hands and jumped up and down for joy after they did what I told them not to do when they were little . . . WHEW!

Peer pressure affects everyone but especially young people because they are more vulnerable. If you throw in "home alone" kids (those who come home to an empty house for a good part of the day) and mixed messages (the do this, but if you can't, then do this, first best, second best, scenario), then the pressure is intensified! As we get older, we are not as subject to peer pressure because we have a greater sense of who we are and where we are going. We've also formed our consciences (and that last word could be the source for another whole book!). One of the best stories I ever heard regarding peer pressure is a true one. There was a woman who had reached the very ripe age of one hundred twenty, and, as she was believed to be the oldest person on earth, the media gathered to interview her. When asked what she liked best about being one hundred twenty, she answered, "There's no peer pressure!"

The term *peer pressure* is such an overused, overrated, exaggerated, and misunderstood concept! Why do I say that? It seems that peer pressure is the stock answer for "what's wrong with kids today"! Many people believe that teens get pregnant because of peer pressure. Peer pressure doesn't cause pregnancy, sex does! Others blame teen drinking and teen drug use on peer pressure, as if the easy availability of alcohol and drugs has nothing to do with it! Make no mistake about it, peer pressure can be a powerful force, but it doesn't always have to be a negative force, and it's certainly not the only force. I think that the term peer pressure has gotten the bum rap, and it's time we look for other answers so that we can come up with real solutions. Here's how I see it. There are more young people today into drugs, alcohol, and premarital sex because of *negative* peer pressure, the easy availability of drugs and alcohol, the commercialization of sex, deception, desensitization, and downright lies!

I urge all of you to do something to help turn peer pressure into a positive force. If peer pressure can be used to try and talk people into doing what's wrong, then why can't it be used to try and talk them into doing what's right? Teens need to understand that very dated phrase, *occasions of sin*. I heard that phrase so often as a teen, and I knew that it meant putting myself in a spiritually dangerous situation, a situation where the temptation to commit a sin would be strong. How can we explain that term to teens today? (Keep in mind that I am not honing in on teens because I think that they are the problem. I spend most of my time speaking to teens because I believe they are our hope for a better tomorrow which will only happen if we start working on today.)

Going to a party at someone's house because his or her parents aren't home and booze will be available is an occasion of sin. Going to a movie that is "R" rated is an occasion of sin. Hearing someone spew obscenities or "talk dirty" is an occasion of sin. Staying to hear more or speaking that way ourselves is a sin, but it takes an informed conscience to know it's a sin. Someone exerting positive peer pressure would say, "I don't feel like going to the party, how about if we do something else." "That movie sounds dumb, let's see something else." "Your language belongs in the gutter, clean it up." Positive peer pressure doesn't mean having to give a moral sermon to your friends, but it should include a positive challenge to do the right thing, and, as I've said all through this book, teens are up to moral challenges.

What's all this got to do with chastity? It has a lot to do with chastity. If people can talk each other into having sexual intercourse, then they can talk each other out of it. Modesty, purity and temperance, the ingredients to chastity, can be practiced because of positive peer pressure, or flaunted because of negative peer pressure. In fact, let's add positive peer pressure as another important ingredient to chastity! *Yes*, this book is about chastity and one of the tools I'm using in it is positive peer pressure. It's all connected—positive peer pressure and chastity are a dynamic duo!

CHAPTER 19

EQUAL BUT DIFFERENT

Some people have asked me what I say at an all boy's high school, the implication being that the message couldn't be the same for them as it is for girls. Ah, but the message is the same no matter the gender, the age, the geographical area, the ethnic background, or the vocation of those in the audience. Chastity is for everyone! I took four years of Latin in high school, which goes back to my father's "Because I said so!" explanation. In Latin class we had to memorize the gender of nouns. Patria, patriae, F(feminine) country, and equus, equi, M(masculine) horse, are two that I still remember. Now that didn't mean that all countries were feminine and all horses were masculine, but each noun did have a gender.

I don't remember whether F or M came after the Latin word for chastity, but the chastity in my message has an F and an M after it! Chastity equally applies to both sexes, even though both sexes are different. I give the same message to the boys as I give to the girls, but I do use different examples in explaining the meaning. I'll get to that later. First, let me explain the equal but different title to this chapter.

God did indeed make us equal. Therefore, treating either sex as inferior to the other must never be tolerated. Over the years, women have had to fight hard for the right to vote; the right to hold public office; the right to be hired, promoted, and paid according to their talents; and in today's society, the right to stay home and raise their children. Women should never be forced into servitude, but when women choose to serve others as mothers, wives, sisters, and teachers, such service is invaluable. The greatest woman ever born was not famous for her lucrative salary or high position in the work force, but rather for her humility and her willingness to serve. When told by an angel that she was chosen to be the mother of God, Mary answered, "I am the handmaid of the Lord, be it done unto me according to thy word." The word handmaid might offend some women today, but if it is looked at in the context of this passage, it should become a goal and a challenge for all women. No matter a woman's vocation or status in life, if she seeks to serve the Lord by serving others, she is imitating Mary the Mother of God, and for role models, you can't do better than that!

Some women will serve the Lord as presidents of corporations. Some will serve the Lord as politicians and, perhaps someday, as presidents of this country. Other women will serve the Lord as religious sisters, or lay women active in the church. Many will serve the Lord as mothers of families: changing diapers, nurturing children, teaching them how to talk and walk and to know, love, and serve the Lord. Over the years there has been a downgrading of motherhood because it lacks the monetary status of other jobs that women could be doing if they weren't "stuck at home with kids." I don't write this to insinuate that all women feel this way, but some do because they have felt the financial crunch and the ridicule that sometimes comes with the decision to stay at home. Motherhood, while it is not the vocation of all women, is an honor and a privilege for those who have been called to it and who have answered, "I am the handmaid of the Lord, be it done according to thy word." I can hear some of you thinking (Mothers do develop that extra sense of hearing, along with eyes in the back of our heads!), "Molly doesn't think all women who have children actually say that does she?" No, but saying it doesn't matter, living it does. Make no mistake about it, being open to the gift of life involves trusting in the Lord, and, in those very difficult and trying circumstances, it takes a real surrender to His awesome love.

Some people think that because male and female are equal, that makes us the same. There's no doubt that we are both made to God's image and likeness, but we are different. My children lost their Daddy when they were very young, but I never said to them, "Don't worry kids, I'll become your mother and your father." I couldn't because Jim and I were different, and some of that difference had to do with his maleness and my femaleness. As a father and as a man, Jim loved our children, played with them, disciplined them, and taught them about God in his own way. I did those things too, but in my own way, as a woman and a mother. Is this subject worth a whole chapter? I believe it is because if we do not recognize the differences in each other as male and female, then we cannot appreciate or respect those differences. Remember, chastity is rooted in respect.

God made only two sexes. Hey, He's God which means He could have made as many as He wanted! God chose to create us in His image and likeness as male or female, and He chose to allow us, His creation, to participate in His act of creation! What an awesome gift from an awesome God! I am so grateful that He allowed me and my husband Jim to work together with His creative plan to have eight children, eight gifts, eight constant reminders of Jim's love for me, and the Father's love for me. Procreation was part of God's plan when He made two sexes, and when He instituted the Sacrament of Matrimony. Children are the fruits of that sacred sexual union. The value of a child is never diminished because he or she is born out of wedlock, and, as people of God, we need to reach out to women in unplanned, crisis pregnancies, but chastity places the sexual act and procreation in marriage.

Another reason for male and female being equal but different is so that we can help each other get to Heaven. Salvation belongs to our God, but because of the gift of free will, the acceptance or rejection of that salvation belongs to us. We cannot merit salvation. It was gained for us on the cross, but God loves us so much that He does not impose salvation on us, we must choose it. Men and women have different gifts, different talents, different personalities, and different capabilities, and we can use these differences to help each other come closer to God and to remind each other constantly of God's awesome forgiveness and mercy when we stray from the path of salvation. I always tell my kids that their father and I made a pact when we got married that we would help each other get to Heaven and that their dad just beat me to it. Jim's there! I'm going! My kids are going to get in too, because when I get there, I'm going to badger God and bend His ear until He lets them in—after all, that's what mothers do! I'm just being silly when I say that, but there is truth in it. A mother and a father, if they take God's word seriously, are called to help each other and to help their children accept salvation by rejecting sin.

In the schools, when I am addressing this equal but different concept, I tell students that a girl has a strong love drive and a boy has a strong sex drive, and that love and sex are not the same thing. I also tell them that a girl physically matures at an earlier age while a boy sexually matures at an earlier age. If sex is reduced merely to the physical act, then what is looked on as affection by a girl might cause arousal in the boy. This is never to insinuate that girls can control their sexual desires better than boys. That's simply not true! Whether we are male or female, our main reproductive organ is our brain! The brain is the control center for most of our actions. Males and females have the same ability to control themselves, and they must both respect each other and understand their differences. If she teases him and thinks that he will respond as she would, she's fooling herself. If he pressures her and thinks that she will respond as he would, he's fooling himself . . . and teasing and pressure have nothing to do with love.

I once spoke at a very elite, private academy for young men, and I was told in advance that the assembly might be tough. Guess what? It wasn't! In fact, the boys were wonderfully receptive. At the end of the talk, I used this example. I told them that although marriage is not for everyone, and that the single life and religious life are also vocations that some of them may be called to, a good number of them would probably marry. I asked them to think about marriage, and if that was to be their vocation, to think about the girl they would marry. I said to them, "Some of you who will marry have not yet met your future wife, but she's out there somewhere, and she's dating someone else! What if you got to meet the fellow who is now dating your future wife?

What would you say to him? Would you care how he treated her? Would you want him to pressure her into having sex with him? Or, would you tell him to keep his hands off her because she is your future wife and that he should show her the utmost respect?" Let me tell you, those young men told me by their body language and facial expressions that respect is what any and all guys better give their future wives.

In an all-girl audience, I often ask this question. "Who holds the upper hand in a relationship, the guy or the gal?" I ask the girls to raise their hands if they think it is the boy. Invariably, very few hands go up. Then I ask a show of hands of those who think it's the girl, and just about every hand goes up! I ask the few who think it's the boy to tell me why they think so, and the answer usually has to do with the fact that boys are physically stronger. I point out that strength shouldn't give a boy any edge unless the girl is afraid of the boy, and who wants to date someone you are afraid of? To say the girl holds the upper hand isn't to say that she is better, or has more control, or that he needs controlling. It has to do with being equal but different!

Chastity is for both sexes, but I firmly believe that it will only take root in our society if women work to make it take root. The girl has always set the boundary lines in a relationship, and although boys and girls are equally responsible for their actions, it's always the girl who has more to lose when it comes to consequences. Oh to be sure, there are spiritual and emotional consequences that affect them both, but the physical consequences of a sexual relationship take a greater toll on the girl—only women get pregnant! All forms of contraception, except one, are meant to be ingested, injected, or inserted in females, and now that there is a female condom, the boy need only worry about his own safety. All abortions are performed on women, never on men. Sexually transmitted diseases are more damaging to a woman's reproductive organs because they are inside of her! I never want to paint sex as something bad or harmful, but irresponsible sex does have consequences, and the women will bear the brunt of most of those consequences. That's why I ask girls to be honest with themselves and to admit that they do indeed set the boundary lines on a date, and that if they say no, and he keeps going, then he is abusing her or raping her. Women do not ask to be raped, but sadly some girls never learn to set boundary lines, and date rape can be the consequence. Most colleges and universities have seminars on date rape for incoming students, to give them an awareness of what it is and how it can happen. It is also a fact that alcohol is often involved in many date rape cases.

As I crisscross the country, I tell young people about the True Love Waits Program, and their response to it has been overwhelmingly positive. This program came out of the Baptist Church and has spread like wildfire throughout the entire United States! Catholics, Protestants, and even some public schools have adopted this program which invites young people to see their sexuality as a God-given gift and to see chastity as the directions on how to use and enjoy that gift. In the public schools that use this program, the word God is deleted, but the chastity message remains intact. The program's purpose is to have young people, both boys and girls, take a pledge to be chaste. The wording of the pledge may differ somewhat, but the intent is always to invite them to practice chastity. There is not a different pledge for the boys than there is for the girls. The chastity word is both feminine and masculine! At youth rallies I bring pledge cards with me and offer them at the end of my talk. I never pass them out. I invite the young people to come up to me if they want a pledge card, and I always tell them that they can have as many as they want so they can give them to their friends. I usually bring 500 to 1000 cards with me, and I always go home with none!

Here's the wording of the pledge I use.

> *Believing that true love waits, I make a commit-*
> *ment to God, myself, my family, those I date,*
> *my future spouse, and my children, that I will*
> *always live a chaste life, as a single person or*
> *within a covenant marriage relationship.*
>
> *By* _____

I invite the young people to go home and to think and pray about the pledge before they make their decisions to sign. I also explain to them that everyone can make this pledge, but for some it will involve changing their sexual behavior. If someone has already engaged in premarital sex, signing the pledge is a promise to stop having sex, and to start being chaste! After signing it, I suggest that they put it in a place where they can see it and be reminded constantly of it. (Maybe attach it to the telephone!) I also tell them that it is not a binding contract but rather a sincere promise to the Lord, and I remind them of God's forgiveness and His willingness to allow them to start over if the pledge is broken, but the intent to keep it must be present!

I would urge everyone reading this book to promote the True Love Waits Program. It involves teaching chastity to young men and women and to encourage them to encourage each other to take the chastity pledge.

CHAPTER 20

QUESTIONS I'M
ASKED MOST FREQUENTLY

Let me first explain that the questions I'm referring to are the ones most asked of me by teens. Adults also ask questions, but they more often have to do with my personal life: How did you get started in the ministry? How do you keep such a busy schedule? Why are you so optimistic? Where do you get your energy? Do you think you will ever remarry? This chapter is not about those questions, but I'll repeat what you already know.

God is my fuel. God travels with me. I have great hope because I know that we win in the end! I read the last page! God is always victorious. All we have to be is faithful! As far as marrying again, I am still very much in love with Jim Kelly and am looking forward to a heavenly reunion. Jim is still very present in my life, and I am still very much Mrs. James D. Kelly.

Now onto the four questions asked most frequently by teens, and let me insert here that I think they are very fair questions and deserve fair and straightforward answers.

QUESTION 1—HOW FAR SHOULD I GO?

When young people ask this question, they are seeking boundary lines. If a son or daughter asks a parent this question and gets this question in return, "How far have you gone?"!!! then this might be the last time the teen turns to his or her parents for answers to frank questions. Parents should not prejudge their children because they are asking a provocative question. So many times young people will come up to me and say, "I can't talk to my parents about sex because as soon as I bring it up, they think I've done it." Remarks that parents make to their children can cause them to go elsewhere for help in an unplanned pregnancy, and sometimes that help can be an abortion clinic. Teens have said to me, "My parents would kill me if I got pregnant." What they really mean is, "My parents would be so hurt if I got pregnant," and to spare parents the hurt, their children often have their grandchildren killed. I believe with all my heart that the vast majority of parents love their children and would help them through difficult situations, but parents need to let their children know that they will always be there for them, no matter what! It's okay to let our kids know that their actions do indeed hurt us because we love them so much, and we want them to be happy, but parents need to get over the hurt and get to the help as quickly as possible. Planned Parenthood and other family planning clinics tell young people that it doesn't matter how far they go as long as they are using contraception, which in essence are the tools to fornicate. Planned Parenthood dispenses contraceptives, including the prescription birth control pill, to teenagers, and parents do not have to give permission. Planned Parenthood is also the largest single provider of abortions in the world, and offers abortion as a solution to those who become pregnant because they have gone too far, and perhaps relied on "safe sex" products that failed. Keep in mind that there is no product or procedure involved in practicing chastity and, therefore, no cost involved, no signed permission slip needed, and it's 100 percent effective! Could it be that chastity might just put some organizations right out of business?

Who loves our young people the most? It's my belief that parents love their children the most, but they need to communicate that love by being open to answering any and all kinds of questions in as nonjudgmental a way as possible and by being there for their children in any and all circumstances. Unconditional love and forgiveness are what God offers His children and what He wants us to offer our children.

"How far should I go?" I use the example of a truck driver driving down a hill and seeing a huge branch in the middle of the road. Does the truck driver wait until right before the tree to begin to apply the brakes, or does the truck driver begin to apply the brakes as soon as he sees the danger? The answer is obvious, and it applies to the "How far should I go" question. I explain in my talks that there is a difference between affection and arousal. Affection can include hugging, holding hands, and kissing—and it's reserved for special people in our lives. If we show affection to everyone, even those we really don't know, then it loses it's meaning. In Hollywood films, we can see people kiss in the back of a cab and then say, "Hi, my name is Sally, what's yours?" This kind of so-called affection is meaningless.

When the boundary lines of affection are crossed, arousal is the result. Petting, necking, and prolonged kissing are all part of foreplay, and foreplay is a prelude to sexual intercourse. If someone crosses the line from affection to arousal, the brakes do not work as well, and if alcohol is involved, the results can be deadly! Boundary lines need to be set, talked about, and honored by the guy and the gal. One girl once said to me, "If we are already into petting and necking, you don't really think we can stop, do you?" I said, "What if your parents walked in?" to which she replied, "I'd stop!" My point was to say that you can stop if you understand where control comes from, but you make it harder to stop when you cross the boundary line.

Some young people have shared with me their disappointment in the sexual act. They went "all the way" because they felt it was expected of them by their date, or that they would lose their boyfriend or girlfriend if they didn't do it. Some young people have bought into the lie that "everyone's doing it." Some do it out of curiosity, because they have been tempted, teased, and titillated by sexual messages and want to find out for themselves what it's like. Many who engage in sexual intercourse are looking for love, and, because they have substituted the word sex for love, they find out the hard way that those words are not synonyms. How sad that some young people have a bad view of sex because they went too far, too soon, and feel hurt and used because of it. God placed foreplay and sexual intercourse in marriage because it is rooted in commitment, fidelity, mutual trust, and an openness to the gift of children. Outside of marriage, there can be fleeting pleasure, but lasting pain. If someone has had sex outside of marriage, he or she should be invited to become a "born again" virgin! Secondary virginity is possible because of God's grace and forgiveness.

Speaking of grace, that is the key to practicing chastity. Some people in society want to give kids the tools to have sex, when all they really need are the tools to say *no* to premarital sex and *yes* to chastity. These tools consist of communication skills, positive peer pressure, and God's grace! Grace is a hard word for young people because it is conceptual rather than concrete. In other words, they can't buy it at a store or send for it in a catalogue, and they won't see any commercials on national t.v. promoting it. Stay tuned for my formula for grace getting!

QUESTION 2—HOW DO I SAY NO?

This is the most-asked question. If answered truthfully, it would save a lot of young people the painful consequences of saying yes to premarital sex. Far too many people think that saying no only involves a voice message. In reality, we communicate three different ways—verbally, with body language, and with what I call clothes language. I ask kids if they ever asked their mom or dad for something, and although they got no for an answer, it was really a "maybe," or "ask me later," or the real tip-off that a yes is coming, "We'll see." All of the young people knew what I meant and told me that they could tell when a parent's no was a real no, or when with prodding and persistence from them, it could be turned into a yes! That's a good example because then teens can realize that their *no* to someone who is coming on strong to them could also be interpreted as a maybe or a yes.

I tell them that if they mean no then they have to communicate it by the tone of their voice. They don't have to yell it, but they do have to say it in a way that is clearly a "No. Don't ask me again! I'm worth waiting for and if you don't think so, bug off!" It sounds harsh, but sometimes a firm *no* can establish those boundary lines, and make dating an enjoyable experience rather than a time to worry about what he or she is going to try next.

Do people really have body language? You bet they do! As

the mother of eight children, five of whom were teens at the same time, I can assure you that body language is real, it's loud, and it's easily interpreted. Every time I served meatloaf, I was greeted by my kids' negative body language. Without ever saying a word, their bodies told me that meatloaf was not a favorite menu item in our house.

I often think of the fourth Station of the Cross where Jesus meets His Mother on the way to His crucifixion. What did they say to each other? We aren't told, but I believe that there was complete silence, and yet their eyes conveyed the deep sorrow and tremendous love they had in their hearts for each other. I love a hymn called, "Be still and know that I am God." When I go before the Blessed Sacrament in Eucharistic adoration, my body language, kneeling in silent prayer, says to God, "I love you!"

There is no doubt about it, girls or guys can say no with their lips but yes with their eyes or hands. I remind young people that if they mean no, then they need to communicate that with their whole body, and that if the person they are with leaves them because they said no, then that person doesn't love them anyway. It can hurt to lose someone, but it sure does speak volumes about the person who does the leaving, and it can save a lot of pain later on. Obviously, if that's why they left, then they will go and find someone else to pressure into having sex, and that's not the kind of person someone would want to marry. Saying no to premarital sex is saying, "I'm worth waiting for, and marriage is what I'm waiting for!" This book is for people of all ages, people who are single, engaged to be married, or married. The message is the same. Sexual intercourse belongs in marriage and only in marriage, and if one never marries, then one should never engage in sexual intercourse. We live in a society where some have equated sex with food and water! In other words, some people actually think that it is cruel, unhealthy, and downright unnatural to expect someone never to engage in sexual intercourse. The problem is that they have *need* and *desire* mixed up. We have a need for food and water to stay alive, but we do not have a need for sexual intercourse, and no one has ever died abstaining from it. Sometimes I suggest to my audience that they check out the obituaries in the newspaper and see if any of them say, "John Doe, died Sept. 19, 1996, Cause of death: Abstinence!" No, we can't die from refraining from sexual intercourse, but people have died from having sex! It is a known fact that the AIDS virus is often transmitted through sexual encounters.

As far as clothes language, I would invite you to go back to the chapter on modesty. Suffice it to say, we make a statement by what we wear. I point out that Madonna, the singer, makes a statement by what she almost wears, and it is a sexual statement. I like to hold up the real Madonna, the Mother of God, as the best role model for everyone.

How do you say no? Say it firmly with your voice, communicate it with your body and your clothes, and it will never be misinterpreted!

QUESTION 3—WHAT IF I NEVER MARRY?

I answered that under Question 2 when I discussed sexual need and sexual desire. It is important to realize that our sexual desire is always greater than our sexual need, and that desire comes under the control factor. We can desire to eat chocolate until it comes out of our ears, but if we do that, we will get very sick (and have funny looking ears!). We do not have a need for chocolate, just a desire. Someone can desire to punch someone else in the nose, but that desire should be curbed because it is not nice and because the one who throws the punch is likely to get punched in return. Sometimes we want to shoot off at the mouth and tell someone off, but if we control that desire, we are better off. There is a huge difference between sexual desire and sexual need. If we understand the difference, then the single life will be not only a valid vocation, but a real gift to those who are called to it. Some of the most unselfish people I have ever met are single people who have devoted their lives to helping others.

QUESTION 4—HOW WILL WE
KNOW IF WE ARE COMPATIBLE?

Young people point to the soaring divorce rate and wonder what has happened to happy marriages. I was in a school in Canada, and a young man stood up after my talk and boldly declared that he believed the divorce rate would go down if people had sex while they were dating in order to find out if they were sexually compatible. He even used the words "try out someone." If looks could kill, then the girls in the audience were already planning his funeral. I tried to tell him that one of the reasons for the high divorce rate was because so many people had engaged in premarital sex, and, therefore, marital sex for some was no big deal. I never want to embarrass a student, or put down any question or comment, but sometimes the answer has to be blunt. I told him that we can try out products to see if we like them, maybe even take them home on a conditional basis, and buy them if they fit our needs. Most people that buy a car test drive a few before choosing the one they want to spend their time driving. People are not products, however. People are not for sale, and they are not to be tried out or test driven. Dating couples will find out if they are compatible by becoming best friends, and that involves sharing dreams and ideas, spending time just walking and talking, and praying together. If a couple loves each other enough to wait until their wedding night to enjoy that special gift of sexual intimacy then the odds are that they will find a blissful sexual compatibility.

If someone has experienced sex with different people before marriage, then a comparison of lovemaking is almost inevitable, and the relationship will suffer. Again, secondary virginity is always possible, and the sooner one starts over at chastity, the better their marriage will be. Sexual intercourse does not define marriage or a relationship, but it sure can ruin one if sex is the main attraction.

Let me sum up this chapter with some basic answers to all of these questions. Stick with affection and don't stray into the arousal stage. Say no with your whole being, and then you will be saying yes to chastity. Put your vocation decision in God's hands and trust that He will lead you where He wants you to go. If you do not marry, your sexuality will remain intact! Always look at others as temples of the Holy Spirit, and that will keep you from ever seeing others as products to be used and discarded for the sake of pleasure.

CHAPTER 21

MIRACLES!

My purpose in writing this book is to teach, preach, and share the chastity message—and to invite you to do the same. I also want to witness to you God's incredible faithfulness! God uses His people to complete His work on earth, and He equips us with the necessary tools to complete whatever task He's called us to. I don't want anyone who reads this book to say, "I could never do that!" Not everyone is called to travel the world and speak on chastity, but everyone is called to give and live the chastity message. All it takes is a yes to God, and He will do the rest! It's worth repeating, *God blesses yeses!*

Over the course of my ministry, I have been asked umpteen times when I was going to write a book, and although the idea appealed to me, I never felt I had the time it would take to do so. That sentence might make you think that I now have the time! Nope, I don't, and that's what makes this book a miracle! I am busier than ever because chastity is "catching on," and, consequently, I have so many requests to speak that if I accepted them all, I'd have enough frequent flier miles to circle the world . . . three times! "At His pace, with His grace" is my motto, and this book was written with Him, for Him, and coauthored by Him, according to His time schedule!

I want to share with you some miraculous happenings that have occurred in my life since I said "yes" to God's invitation to "Speak the truth in love." My reason for sharing them is twofold. The first reason is because they happened, and I want to give thanks to God publicly for His awesome goodness. The second reason is to ask all of you to think about the miraculous things that have happened in your life, and to share them with others. Some people talk about coincidences, or good luck being involved in events they can't explain, and they fail to recognize God's hand in those events. God wants to perform miracles in our lives, but we need to ask Him to do so, and then let Him loose! I know that I have often gotten in God's way and, because I learned the hard way that I was not Superwoman, I surrendered to Him. In a battle when one side surrenders to the other, the surrendering side is considered the loser, but not so with God. In surrendering to God we put Him in charge, and He becomes our armor, our ammunition, our strength, and our guide.

I already shared with you that I never spoke in public before my husband's death. In college, I majored in business economics, and in my senior year I had to lead a seminar on the theory of supply and demand. I was so nervous that even the professor felt sorry for me as I stammered, stuttered, and stumbled my way through statistical data. Now I speak to thousands of people each week, on moral data, and if that doesn't merit miracle status, then nothing does!

Let me share with you some more of the miracles that God has wrought in Molly Kelly's life, and this is not to impress you with Molly Kelly, but rather it is to impress on you the power of the Holy Spirit.

A few years ago, I received a call from a woman in New Jersey who was the sister of a priest in Rome. She told me that her brother wanted to contact me about a speaking engagement, so I gave her my address and didn't think any more about it. The next thing I knew, I was officially invited to speak to 6000 priests in Rome, Italy, at a world-wide retreat! I went, I spoke, and I consider that invitation a miracle that ranks right up there with the loaves and the fishes! My sister Alice went with me, and she considers it a miracle in her life too. Alice has fifteen children, and I have eight, so just being able to get away was a miracle in itself! During that trip Alice and I had the unexpected privilege of privately meeting with Mother Teresa, who herself is a miracle! Mother Teresa took my hand and said to me, "You are more in love with your husband now than ever, aren't you." Whew! Another miracle! God allowed me to feel Jim's presence through the presence of Mother Teresa. And speaking of saintly people, I also had the awesome experience of meeting Our Holy Father,

Pope John Paul II, and my sister and I both had the privilege of receiving the Holy Eucharist from his hands!

I told the 6000 priests about my mission to spread the chastity message, and I urged each one of them to also speak about chastity from the pulpit, in the mission fields, in the classrooms, during retreats, and anywhere else that their priestly ministry took them. I have spoken to many audiences but never to one as receptive and loving as those 6000 men of God. After my talk they stood and applauded, and, as I came down the aisle, several of them came out and shook my hand. One of them said to me, "I could sense your husband's presence as you spoke." My sister and I will never forget what we call our "Rome Miracle"!

When Jesus walked the earth, He cured the lame, gave sight to the blind, drove out demons, and even brought people back from the dead, not to mention His feat of walking on water and calming the seas! These are miracles that are easily recognized as such by everyone. Even nonbelievers can't explain them, so they either ignore them or shrug them off as the workings of a very clever man some 2000 years ago. The things that I call miracles might not seem as miraculous as these, but in my mind they are! Jesus is still working miracles and He continues to invite us, His modern-day disciples, to be the channels through which His miraculous powers flow. Don't look for events that defy gravity. Instead, let's look at the ordinary things in our lives and watch how God can make them extraordinary!

My next miracle took place in Chicago, at a Marian Conference given to honor and praise the Mother of God and to ask her to intercede for us before the throne of her Son. I have been asked by different people why I have a great devotion to the Mother of God. Some have even asked, "Why go to Mary when you can go directly to Jesus?" I answer that I do go directly to Jesus, but I also go to Him through Mary, and it has to do with my motherhood. I am the mother of six sons, and I know that if someone wanted a favor from one of my boys, they would be smart to go through me. To Jesus through Mary . . . it worked at Cana, and it still works today!

During my talk at the conference I was remarking that if Catholics really grasped the real presence of Jesus in the Eucharist, there would be lines outside of every church every morning to receive Him. My next words, which were written on my notes, were to be, "There are lines at Disney World to go into the haunted house!" But that's not what came out of my mouth. Instead, I said, "There are lines at Disney World to go on Mr. Toad's Wild Ride!" I don't know why I said it, but because it really is a ride at Disney World, I just figured it slipped out. After my talk, a woman came up to me and said, "Thanks so much for your talk. I felt deeply touched by it. Just this week I told God that my spiritual life was like Mr. Toad's Wild Ride." At first I was floored by her remark, but the more I thought about it, the more I realized how God speaks through us when we are open to His proddings. Before every talk I ask God to speak through me, so why should I be so surprised when He does?

This next miracle was a daylong one! I was on my way to the airport to leave for a two-week speaking tour in Australia. I am a homebody and do not like to be away from home for more than two days at a time, so this trip was already weighing heavy on me, and I hadn't even left yet. My daughter Molly drove me to the airport and was going to wait with me until I boarded. I got up to the gate, gave my ticket and passport to the airline representative, and was greeted with the question, "Mrs. Kelly, could I please have your visa?" I looked at her and said, "I don't have a visa. The ticket was sent to me by the people who arranged my trip, and they never mentioned the word visa!" The ticket agent looked up and curtly replied, "You need a visa to go to Australia and if you do not have one, you cannot go." Needless to say, I was not feeling calm at this moment. I tried to tell her that this trip had been planned for a year, and that I had twenty-eight speaking engagements involving 15,000 people. In no way do I mean to sound judgmental, but in telling it like it is, I do have to say that this particular ticket agent was rude and very unsympathetic, which didn't help my mood much. My daughter watched as I turned pale, and she said, "Mom, what will you do?" I told her that I was going to call my contact person in Australia, and, in doing so, I found out that it was 2:00 A.M. there! The somewhat groggy person on the other end of the line was extremely concerned but could do nothing until morning, and my plane was about to leave in fifteen minutes! I left out one other little nuance to this story. In packing, I changed pocketbooks because I was changing seasons and going from summer in Philadelphia to winter in Australia, and in doing so I somehow forgot to put in the envelope containing the cash for this trip. So, there I am at the airport, with no visa, no cash, and the boarding announcement had already been given. I told the agent that because my ticket would take me to Houston, and then on to Los Angeles before I changed planes to get to Australia, that I did not need a visa to get on the plane. She took my ticket, stamped it "No Documents," gave it back to me, and again warned me that I would not get to Australia. Talk about a leap of faith. This leap was 35,000 feet high.

I got on the plane and proceeded to pray my way to Houston—nonstop! I told God that I had no idea what He had in store for me, but I was completely depending on His will. I got off at Houston and immediately heard an announcement that the plane for Los Angeles was now boarding. This was not the plane I was to take as I had a four-hour layover in Houston, but I knew God wanted me on that earlier plane. I ran to the phone, called my daughter, and asked her to give me the phone number of a priest friend of mine in Los Angeles. This priest, Father Tom Cusack, is an extremely humble and holy man who travels throughout California giving missions. The fact that he was home, and that I was able to speak to him in that ten minute time frame was part of this daylong miracle. I told him that I was on my way to Australia via Los Angeles and that I needed a visa . . . today! He told me to call him back in ten minutes. I asked the ticket agent in Houston if I could get on this earlier plane and was told yes, but that I still could not get to Australia. She saw the "No Documents" stamp! I called Father Cusack, got a busy signal, and was told to board the plane or miss it. Another leap of faith!

This time I prayed my way across mountains, over the Grand Canyon, and all the way to Los Angeles. I gave it over to the Lord. He knew I had no money and no return ticket if I wasn't allowed to go to Australia. I got off the plane and was greeted by the warmest smile I have ever seen. It was on the face of Father Tom Cusack. He hugged me and, in his delightful Irish brogue, he said, "Come on Molly, we have some places to go." He drove me to the photo place where I got a picture for a visa, and then to the Australian consulate. Not too many cities have an Australian consulate, but Los Angeles does. We got there by 3:00 P.M.; I had my visa by 4:00 P.M.; and I was on the plane to Australia by 7:00 that evening because God came to me through Father Cusack. There is one more thing that I want to point out. The consulate closed at 4:00 P.M. and if I had not taken the earlier plane, I would never have made it in time. If I did not get off at that particular gate in Houston, I would not have heard the announcement for the earlier plane. This is a long story, but it is worth telling because it merits miracle status in my book!

One more quick miracle. I was a banquet speaker in Pittsburgh, and I was feeling sick. It turned out that I had pleurisy, but at that point I didn't know what I had, just that I had something! I was going to give a talk that I had given before, so I felt that I could get through it. I also wanted to tailor the talk for this audience, so I wrote a five-minute introduction that would apply to this particular event. I got up and started to speak and found myself very uncomfortable with the first five minutes because they were new to me and weren't on the tip of my tongue. I was very anxious to get through them and was even tempted to skip the opening and get right into the comfort zone, but I didn't. After my talk, a young woman came up to me and handed me a folded piece of paper. I was sitting with my back to her when she handed it to me, and when I turned to say something to her, she had already gone. I opened the paper and it said, "Mrs. Kelly, thank you for your talk, and especially for the first five minutes of your talk, which really spoke to my heart." That miracle was sent to me special delivery, and that young woman was God's messenger!

I have more miracles that I could share, and I may someday write a book just on the miracles God has worked in my life, but I'll end this chapter with the words from a clipping I once saw taped to someone's refrigerator: "Don't tell God how big your mountain is. Tell your mountain how big your God is!" Our God is still moving mountains, calming seas, and performing all kinds of miracles, but we need to open our eyes, our ears, and our hearts to Him so that He will allow us to not only see miracles, but to also become part of them! God told us to ask and we shall receive . . . why not ask for miracles!

CHAPTER 22

THE WIND BENEATH MY WINGS

In the beginning of the book I talked about what "fueled" me, and I told you that it was first and foremost the Eucharist, which I have the privilege of receiving almost every morning at Mass. In this day and age of high costs and inflation, the greatest banquet ever spread is still free and offered daily all over the world. It is free to us, but it is at such a great price to Jesus. If we were invited by a diplomat or a celebrity to attend a special banquet, we would jump at the invitation. We would also prepare for that special event by getting all spruced up. That's what we should do for the banquet of the Lord. We should go to the Sacrament of Reconciliation and spruce up our souls by getting rid of those stains caused by our sinful nature. Some people think that confessing our sins is only necessary if the stain is a big one—a serious sin. Would we go to any other banquet with just small stains on our clothes? We are going there to meet, greet, and eat the body of Jesus Christ our Savior, who is present body, blood, soul, and divinity in that consecrated host, and that calls for bleach! The grace we receive in the Sacrament of Reconciliation whitens, brightens, and readies our souls to receive our King. My fuel is my Lord, but He's your Lord also and there's plenty of Him to go around!

I did not write this book just for Catholics, and that's the beauty of our God, because He's not just for Catholics. Our God is the God of everyone. I love my Catholic faith and especially the gift of the Sacraments, therefore I share with you as a Catholic. Because we are all brothers and sisters in Christ, I also share with you as a child of God. God's mercy and forgiveness transcends all denominations. He died on the Cross for everyone including those who do not know Him, love Him, or serve Him. This book is an attempt to teach and spread the chastity message, but because God is the Author of that message, I am writing this book to give honor and glory and praise to Him—and to share Him with others.

I told you that my main fuel is the Eucharist, but I also get energized by the people I meet, especially the young people. Over the years I have learned what it is that young people want from a speaker, and it comes down to honesty, sincerity, and not being boring. I think those are fair expectations, and, if met, I find teens a fair and receptive audience.

Let me share with you some of my "people fuel," and some of that "wind," and I'll start out with a blustery high octane story! I was in Iowa and had just spoken to the entire high school student body who were seated (squooshed was more like it!) in the gymnasium. Now a gym is not always the best place to speak, but it can work in my favor because I cheer them on to chastity! After my talk, which I always end by issuing them the challenge to be chaste, a young man came up to me. He told me that he really enjoyed my talk and wanted to know if I had a video of it. I told him I did, but quipped, "Why do you want a video, you just saw the real thing!" He smiled and then said, "You remind me of my mother. She died in May, and I want my little brother to hear what she would have told him." Let me tell you, as the mother of six sons I was deeply moved, and I put my arms around him and just hugged him. That incident alone gave me a month's worth of fuel!

Another time I was speaking in Michigan, and again it was in the gym to the whole school. I was about five minutes into my talk when I heard some laughing, and I hadn't said anything funny yet. Then I noticed a balloon coming up from the stands, and it was being batted from row to row. It took me only a few seconds to realize that it was an inflated condom and that I had to do something quick or the assembly would get out of control. I put my talk on cruise control, which means my mouth kept spouting words, but my mind was racing to find the right words for this present dilemma. In times like this I rely heavily on the Holy Spirit, and my dependence always pays off. My first thought was to scold them, after all I am a mother and that's what I would have done to my own kids. I realized that they would then connect chastity with the day that they all got in trouble, and chastity would forever have a negative connotation for them. The thought crossed my mind to simply ask them to hand me the balloon, but then the Chastity Lady would be standing in front of 1000 kids, holding an inflated condom. I quickly dismissed that thought. Finally, I allowed the Holy Spirit to kick in and here's what I said, "You know, some things are funny, but I know that if any one of you were holding your best friend's hand as he or she was dying from AIDS, I'll bet you wouldn't laugh, and I'll bet you wouldn't hand them a condom." There was an abrupt silence, and the balloon disappeared. When I tell that story, I've been asked how I thought up such a clever answer. I answer, "I didn't think it up, it was the Holy Spirit's idea."

People have asked me if I ever have hard days. I've been in some difficult situations, that last one being one of them, but I've never been laughed off the stage or asked to leave. I am extremely impressed with young people today, and, although I believe that all of them are worth the chastity message, I know that all of them will not listen or like it. I also know that I am giving a life-saving message and, therefore, if only one life is saved by it, my entire ministry is worth it. Sometimes I remind myself that although Jesus died to save everyone, He would have gone through the entire crucifixion for just one person.

Many people ask me how I measure my success. In other words, how do I know if they listen? Do I take surveys a few months later? Do I give the students pre-tests and post-tests? What is my evaluation process? While all of these are important tools, I use none of them. Some have dismissed me as a "one shot deal." She comes, she speaks, she leaves. To be honest, however, there is often controversy before I come and a rippling effect after I leave. The controversy usually stems from fears that I might start "talking religious" in a public school, that kids will act up in the assembly, or that the "other side" will have to be invited in.

I would like to address these fears in case any of you hear them. I do not say God's name or speak in religious terms in a public school, but I do give God's message. In Catholic and Christian schools I will say that sexual intercourse belongs in marriage where God intended it to be. In public schools I will tell the kids to place sexual intercourse in marriage where it belongs. Same message said differently. I am not afraid to say God, but if I did, it would shut the door to any future assemblies on chastity. Do you see how important it is that we get God reenrolled in the public schools? My rule of thumb is to say God's name openly where I can and to quietly pray His name where I can't. Either way, He comes with me!

As far as the kids acting up, it just doesn't happen unless the school itself demands no discipline, that is extremely rare. If you can make a case for chastity, using humor, stories, and a positive approach, kids are fair. I always tell them that the choice will be their choice, but I do not offer them a mixed message, so the choice comes down to accepting the message or rejecting it. No one likes to feel that they are being forced into something, so I offer chastity as a choice, and the only choice I can offer them because I refuse to offer them anything less than the best!

I remember the time I was speaking in upstate New York, and the principal called and asked if I would arrive fifteen minutes before the assembly because he needed to talk to me. He told me that before I was invited, he showed my videos to different people. The first group consisted of some of the teachers who, after watching it, gave a thumbs down to my speaking at an assembly. They didn't think it was appropriate. The second group was made up of the school nurse and some local health professionals who also shot down the assembly. They didn't think it was appropriate. In the third group were parents and they too said no to an assembly. They didn't think the kids would listen. The principal watched the video again, and on it he heard me say that instead of forming committees to study teen problems, we need to go right to teens with the problems. I also said that teens and adults need to work together on solving the problems, but it will be the teens who make those answers work or not work. The principal, acting on my suggestion, proceeded to form a committee of students, making it as diverse as possible. He told me that one girl on the committee was pregnant. He sat them down and asked them to watch my video and to decide whether or not he should invite this woman (me) to come and address the student body. The principal told me that every single student said, "Yes! Invite her. We deserve to hear this message." And so I came and spoke to the entire school, and the message was well-received. After the assembly, some of the young people came up on the stage to thank me for coming and to tell me, with big smiles on their faces, that they were responsible for my speaking at their school. Can you see why my tank is never on empty?

I'll answer the "We'll have to invite the other side in" fear with the question, "Who is the other side?" If the other side are those who promote the "safe sex" message in the school then I would submit that chastity must be the *other* side! I point out that schools do not offer the other side to drugs, alcohol, smoking, or date rape! Why should they feel they have to offer the other side to chastity and abstinence? Sometimes school officials need to hear these arguments so they can use them to fend off those who want condoms in the curriculum.

I also speak to parents. In fact, I try to do so on every trip. I believe with all my heart that parents are the primary educators of their children, and that the message I give will go nowhere fast if it is not affirmed at home. Let me share with you some parental anecdotes. First, let me tell you that the vast majority of parents respond favorably to the chastity message. I am not bragging but just relating the facts, and standing ovations are the norm for parent assemblies. Why? Parents appreciate that I speak the truth. They love their children and want them to be happy and healthy. I share with parents that all of them want whole and wholesome kids, but why stop there? How about holy kids? If we don't call our own children to holiness, who will? Isn't holiness the secret to health and happiness? Yes it is, and let's not keep it a secret. Let's tell everyone we meet. Let's get those boom and boogie boxes to blast a tune that calls kids to be holy! Slim chance you say? No chance if we don't try, I say!

One parent said to me that she didn't feel she could tell her daughter to practice chastity when she didn't as a teenager. I said to her that some of the best teachers are those who have learned the hard way. I asked her if she ever heard of St. Mary Magdalene and St. Augustine? Mary Magdalene at one time was a prostitute, and Augustine fathered an illegitimate child. But both of them fell in love with God, repented of their sins, and spent the rest of their lives calling others to live pure, holy lives . . . and both of them are saints! I also told her that we do not have to share our sins with our children. Once we confess them, they are forgiven and gone! Why dig them up?

One dad came up to me after my talk and said, "Thanks, I needed that! I was just beginning to cave in on my son by talking about condoms in case he decided to become sexually active. I was beginning to give a mixed message, and I needed to hear from you how deadly and demeaning that is." I gave the example that if a parent knew that the steering wheel on the family car locked 10 percent of the time, would the parent allow the kids to borrow the car? And if the parent did, and the son or daughter was killed because of it, wouldn't the parent feel a sense of guilt over the death? Giving a child a condom, knowing that the median failure rate is 17 percent, is like playing rubber roulette. What if that child contracts the AIDS virus? Wouldn't the parent who urged the child to use a condom feel a deep sense of guilt? If our children, or anyone else for that matter, choose to practice risky behavior, they need to be told that it is dangerous to the health of their souls, minds, and bodies. They need to be challenged to change their behavior. If they continue such behavior and become pregnant or contract a sexually transmitted disease, parents need to forgive them and to help and love them through the difficult times. Let me insert here that I am never equating pregnancy and disease as similar problems. A baby has value regardless of the circumstances of his or her conception. A disease is a sickness and has value only in redemptive suffering.

Many teens have told me that they can't talk to their parents and so they go elsewhere for help and advice. Too often teens turn to Planned Parenthood or other family planning clinics where they are offered the "safe sex" or abortion "solution." What teens are really afraid of is hurting their parents. We need to somehow show our disapproval and disappointment without scaring teens away. They need us at these times more than ever. We are the ones who must be there for them and who must continue to call them to chaste, holy lives.

I can't tell you the number of parents who have come up to me and described some of the hideous things that are being taught in various sex ed classes. One father was distraught as he related to me that his daughter was in a mixed health class and was told to put a condom on the finger of a boy student. I didn't even want to put that in my book, but we must not delude ourselves into thinking that such a thing couldn't happen in *our* school. I am not against public schools, and I have been most impressed with many of the principals, teachers, and students. Because I speak on chastity, however, I review a lot of the material that is being taught in some of the schools. Believe me when I say that some of it is bad! My point in bringing this up is to urge parents to request to see the curriculum dealing with sexuality education, to review it yourself, and then to decide if that is what you want your son or daughter to be taught. If you don't like it, go to the teacher and explain why. If you get nowhere, go to the principal. The best thing to do is to get other parents to go with you. In fact, form a parent group, like the one in New York called PROVE—Parents for the Restoration of Values in Education. You might ask what good this would do. Well, this particular group was successful in not only ousting a very bad curriculum, but also in getting the superintendent of schools ousted because he was hellbent on getting this offensive curriculum in all of the schools in his district. It pays to speak up, and our kids are worth it, but do your complaining in a polite and respectful way. Yelling and screaming will get you nowhere fast. The best thing to do is to bring a positive curriculum with you and suggest that the school get rid of the bad one and use the positive one. There are many good abstinence curricula available. Just make sure that it is 100 percent abstinence, and not abstinence-based. The latter phrase often means that while abstinence is offered as the best solution, the "safe sex" message is also given to protect those kids who are going to "do it" anyway. My name and address are in the back of this book, and if you want a list of good curricula, write me and I'll send it to you. That's the rippling effect I'm hoping for!

I'll sum up this chapter by saying that vigilant parents help produce virtuous kids!

CHAPTER 23

MORE WIND

I have so many more stories to share that I'll spend this whole chapter doing just that . . . telling stories of things that have happened to me over the past fifteen years. I believe that I have been called by God to work in His vineyard, and that it's the young grapes that I am to tend . . . the teens! Teens are the easiest audience and the hardest audience. They are the easiest because they demand nothing next to my name. They are not impressed with how many awards or degrees a speaker has received, where that speaker has been, or who that speaker knows. They are only interested in what you have to say to them and why you are saying it. A speaker could have twenty doctorates and still be judged boring by teens. When I finally learned that about teens, it made me feel confident and comfortable in front of them because I knew that while I wasn't anyone that important, my message was!

Teens are also the hardest audience because they have X-ray vision. They can see right through a speaker, and it only takes them five minutes. If someone is phony, teens have phony detectors. If someone speaks to teens but really doesn't like teens, then the teens are not apt to like the message. I am now training other people to be speakers, and I tell them that the messenger is as important as the message. If you think about it, it's really not what Mother Teresa of Calcutta says but how Mother Teresa lives. Mother Teresa *is* the message. No messenger should give a message unless that messenger lives that message. Teens may disagree with the message, but if it's given fairly and squarely by someone who believes in the message and who believes in them, then the teens will be open to listening. Don't worry about whether or not they will accept the message, that's the Holy Spirit's assignment!

On to the stories, or the wind beneath my wings, as I call them. About a week before I was to speak at a public school, I was sent a newspaper article that was written about my coming to the school. You would think, from the article, that I was going to discuss the benefits of nuclear war! Some people on the school board did not want me to come and decided to get the teens riled up. They talked about this woman coming to force her morality on others and tell kids that sex was bad. The article also quoted the teen editor of the school newspaper as saying, "Molly Kelly will be laughed off the stage." Now others might read that and feel a surge of excitement. I felt sick! My first thought was to cancel. I said to myself, "Who needs this? Why should I put myself in such a negative situation? This is a setup." Then I thought about Christ and His journey to the Cross, and I realized that any discomfort I might experience could not touch what the Pharisees, the Roman soldiers, and all of us did to Him. I went, I prayed, and I didn't conquer, but I also didn't lose the war. The kids were great. They didn't hear what they expected to hear, or what someone else had told them they were going to hear. Oh, I'm sure they listened for it, but I talk fast! I tell them I like them, I use humor, I tell a lot of stories, and the talk was over before they knew it!

After the assembly, the school had a tea and cookie session so that some of the students could come and meet me and talk to me. The editor of the school newspaper (the one who said I would be laughed off the stage) came up to me and said, "You were better than I thought you'd be." I then said to him, "So are you, Kevin!" It was a neat experience.

Another time I was in New York speaking at an evening session, mostly to adults, but some teens were present. There were 600 people in attendance, which is a huge crowd for an evening talk, and I was told that it was due to a flyer that the local family planning center had distributed with actual quotations from my lips. Make no mistake about it, chastity can be scary to those who promote contraception and abortion because if people practice chastity, then they will never need either! Let's face it, chastity could put family planning clinics out of business! I was warned that there were "plants" in the audience and that they would stand up and challenge me during the question and answer period. I prayed for guidance, delivered my talk, and received a standing ovation. When it came time for questions, a physician stood up and said, "Ms. Kelly, I'm afraid that if young people listen to you, they won't use condoms." To which I respectfully replied, "Doctor, if teens listen to me, they won't need condoms." He still wasn't finished. He then said, "What about the teens who won't buy into the chastity message?" A young teenage girl raised her hand, stood, and said, "Doctor, we hear the "safe sex" message all the time in health class. I came to hear her message." Her answer brought down the house. That evening when I was watching the late news, the same doctor was being interviewed about his reaction to my talk, and the media highlighted his bias instead of what really went on that evening. I knew what went on, and I don't know about that doctor, but I really slept well because, once again, a teenager gave me "fuel"!

Here is one of my favorite stories, actually it is two stories in one. In my talk I ask teens how many of them have *not* heard, read, or seen the word *condom* in the past two weeks. Usually two or three hands go up, and I'm talking an average audience of about 800 teens. Next, I ask them to raise their hands if they *have* heard, read, or seen the word *chastity* in the past two weeks. Again, I usually see about three hands go up. I then point out to them that the condom people are obviously doing a better job of advertising. Why? I tell them that it must be because people don't know the word chastity; or, because no one is going to challenge them to do something they don't believe they can do; or, because chastity is not a product. I point out to them that chastity can't be bought or sold, and it can't be made into a pill or a repellent.

Now having told you the usual answers I get, let me share with you two unusual answers. I was in North Dakota, speaking in a crowded gym, and I asked the audience of teens how many had not seen, read, or heard the word condom in the past two weeks, and two hands went up. I then asked them how many had seen, read, or heard the word chastity, and to my complete surprise *every* hand went up, and one girl at the top of the stands was standing up and wildly waving to me. I could not imagine why she was so excited. By this time she was really dancing in the aisle. I finally yelled up to her and asked her what she was doing, and she yelled back, "I'm Chastity!" It was her name!

At a school in Pennsylvania, I asked the same questions and got the same answer for the condom part. When I asked about chastity, one young man put his hand up and, when I called on him, he said, "Isn't chastity part of a car?"

I explain to young people that chastity has to do with self-control not birth control. It has to do with freedom not restriction. Chastity would free them from the worries of getting pregnant; contracting sexually transmitted diseases; feeling used; getting sick from harmful reactions to birth control; feeling guilty, and so much more. Chastity will put these fears to rest because it is 100 percent effective, costs nothing, has no harmful side effects, and no one has ever gotten sick from it! Make no mistake about it, ***purity is security!***

CHAPTER 24

SUMMARY AND "RAP" UP!

Do you remember the "I can't believe I ate the whole thing!" popular ad slogan from a few years ago? Well, that's how I feel about this book . . . I can't believe that this is the last chapter! I often thought about writing a book, but realizing the time it would take to do so, I always put the idea on the back burner and just let it simmer. This summer, the idea began to come to a boiling point! Now this might lead you to believe that I was finally able to write my book because I knew I would be facing a restful and relaxing summer, but not so! This summer was filled with family adventures, speaking engagements, and the unexpected death of my youngest brother, all of which made this *not* the best time to write my book. Ah, but isn't that when God is at His best . . . when we most need Him, and most heed Him! This next sentence isn't about me telling you how good this book is, but it is about me telling you how I felt as I wrote it. This book was divinely inspired!

I began writing this book in a haphazard way. I'd sit at the word processor, type out a few thoughts, and go off and do something else. I did this for a few weeks and found I had twenty-eight pages written. I was psyched! "Wow! Look what *I did*," I said to myself! One morning I got up before dawn and decided to review what I had already written, and it was gone! I had left the disk in the word processor overnight, and a thunderstorm zapped it! Needless to say, I was devastated! I laid across my bed and half decided to hang up my pen! My notes were sketchy at best, and there was no way I could recover those twenty-eight pages. Ah, but the other half of me said, "Satan, I know you do not want this book written because it exposes you for what you are . . . the master deceiver; a liar, liar pants on fire; and you want me to cry uncle, but instead, I am going to cry Abba!" To be perfectly honest with you, from that moment on it was smooth sailing! Oh to be sure, writing was laborious and time consuming, but it was also fun and very fulfilling because I put it all in God's hands.

Once I made the decision not to let anyone or anything deter me from my goal, it was a breeze, and the name of that breeze was the Holy Spirit! Hey, He appeared to the apostles on Pentecost in a whoosh of wind, and every time I sat at the word processor I experienced that whoosh! There were times when I fully expected to look up and see that tongue of fire over my head! So in this final chapter let me give credit where credit is due. I am simply the ghost writer for the Holy Spirit, and every word, on every page, has the same footnote explaining the source! Instead of putting the footnote at the bottom of every page, I'll simply give it to you now.

Footnote for every word in Molly's book: *Holy Spirit*; "Third Person of the Blessed Trinity"; pp. *all!*

I would like to tell you one more story before I end this chapter. Jesus used parables/stories to get His point across, and because we are all called to be Christlike, I wanted to share some of the things that have happened to me as I travel the world trying to get His point across.

A few years ago, I received a letter from Bishop Harry Flynn to speak at a conference for the Roman Catholic Bishops of the United States. Again I was dumbfounded by such an invitation, but I said yes because I knew from past experience that God blesses yeses! The theme of this conference for the shepherds of the church was "Feed My Sheep." As I sat down to write my talk, I asked God what He wanted me to say to the bishops, and I heard Him say, "Feed My Shepherds." I then asked God what He wanted me to feed them, and He said to me, "Feed them what you want them to feed my sheep." I knew that God wanted to tell the bishops and cardinals to speak about the gifts of life and sexuality and to encourage them to be the shepherds that God has called them to be.

I drew a blank when trying to write an opening for my talk. I put it aside for awhile and decided to play a game of chess with my seven-year-old grandson, Brendan, and God used Brendan to give me my opening line. Brendan said to me, "Grandmom, the most important player on the board is the bishop! He can go anywhere, and he protects the queen!" I knew as soon as I heard the words come out of Brendan's mouth that I was to use them. I told the bishops that my seven-year-old grandson had helped me write my talk, and I went on to explain about the chess game and what he said. I then told them that bishops are most important to our church, can go anywhere, and that they do indeed protect the queen—our Holy Mother the Church. God spoke to Moses through a bush, to me through my grandson, and to the bishops through me!

This book is all about chastity and the importance of giving and living the message. It's what I call a linchpin virtue. Take chastity out of our lives and there goes modesty, purity, honesty, integrity, and truth! I can't end the book without giving you the formula necessary to practice chastity. You see, without God's help it is impossible to live a chaste life. Satan lurks everywhere— in television shows, movies, videos, song lyrics, sex education courses, to mention just a few of Satan's favorite haunts! Keep in mind that Satan started out as Lucifer the Archangel, and that it took another Archangel, St. Michael, to defeat such an evil power and to demote him to hell for all eternity. You and I can't win a battle with Satan relying on our own power, but by calling on our own personal guardian angel to protect us, and by using the spiritual weapon given to us by God, we can overcome temptation and live good holy lives. Yes, we will fail sometimes because we rely on our human power rather than God's power, but we always have His forgiveness if we seek it, if we accept it, and if we mean it when we say we are sorry and will try not to commit that sin again.

What is this spiritual weapon that is so powerful it can repel Satan? The weapon is *GRACE*, which translates: God Himself Giving Himself to Us! This sounds all well and good, but how do we get *GRACE*! I end all of my talks in the Catholic and

Christian schools by saying to the young people, "You can't practice chastity without the spiritual tool so let me tell you what it
is and how you get it!" and then I proceed to spell it.

G **Get in touch with God!**—and that's called prayer.
Prayer is simply a conversation with God, and,
like all conversation, it should involve *talking* **and**
listening. God speaks to us in many ways. If we
are aware of His presence, we will hear His voice.
You might even call God a ventriloquist as He can
throw His voice anywhere and speak to us through
anyone, even those who are perceived by others to
be dummies. Sometimes I find myself so busy
asking God for things that I forget the other parts
of prayer—the adoration and thanksgiving part.
Sometimes I forget that God can answer me with
a "No!" Grace allows us to know that God wants
the best for us, and through constant prayer our
store of grace is increased.

R **Reception of the Sacraments and Reading of
Scripture**—As I have repeatedly stated, this book
is for everyone—Catholics, Christians, people of
all faiths, and people of no faith—but it is written
from my Catholic perspective. I am a Catholic,
and I love my Catholic faith. I have a passion for
the Eucharist! When I attend daily Mass and watch
as the priest raises the host, an ordinary piece of
bread, and as I listen to him say, "This is my body
given up for you," I know beyond a shadow of a
doubt that that bread becomes the body of our
Lord and Savior Jesus Christ. People have said to
me, "Molly, how can you be so sure it becomes
the body of Christ? Who told you?" To which I
reply, "the body of Christ!" Jesus Himself told us.
Those are *His* words that the priest is repeating,
and it is through *His* power that that miracle happens thousands of times each day wherever and

whenever the Holy Sacrifice of the Mass is being offered. To be worthy to receive the body of Christ, we need to receive the Sacrament of Reconciliation as often as possible. For me, going to confession can be likened to going to the bank and withdrawing the amount of money needed to get through the week. When we go to the Sacrament of Reconciliation, we withdraw the amount of grace we need to get through each day, and it is always more than enough because God's interest rate only goes up!

As far as the reading of Scripture, that's for everyone! If I told you that there was one book that had all of the answers, wouldn't you want that book? Well that book exists, and it's called Holy Scripture—the word of God.

A   **Avoid the occasions of sin**—To do this, we need to know what sin is. Sin is rejecting God's word, but how will we know God's word if we don't take the time to read it, and how will those in public schools know God's word if He has been expelled? I talked about what the term "occasion of sin" meant in an earlier chapter. To sum it up, if we are not clear on God's word then we will find ourselves smack dab in the middle of sinful situations and unaware of the danger! God's grace sets off a spiritual alarm warning us of the sinful occasion and arming us so that we can avoid falling into sin.

C   **Let your Christianity come first**—If you are a Catholic, let your Catholicism come first. If you are a Lutheran, let your Lutheranism come first; a Baptist, your Baptist faith; and so on. I always tell my teen audience that they can be Illinois Teens, Michigan teens, Pennsylvania teens; and they can be tall teens, short teens, big teens, small teens; and they can be white teens, black teens, hispanic teens, asian teens; but those terms only tell about their place of residence, stature, and ethnic background. Calling yourself a Christian teen tells how you act! We all need to let our faith come first in our lives. I vote as a Christian! That does not mean that I only vote for Christians. It does mean that I vote the Commandments. If a candidate says it's okay to kill unborn babies, and my God says, "Thou shalt not kill," then I'm going with my God! After all, it is a Supreme Being we are all going to go before on Judgment Day, not a Supreme Court Justice! If a candidate says it's okay to distribute condoms in schools, and my God says, "Flee fornication," then that candidate cannot have my vote! What if neither candidate is all you want him or her to be? I need only ask myself if I am all that God wants me to be. If my answer is "not 100 percent," then I have some spiritual growing to do. I don't look at it as the "lesser of two evils theory," but rather in the "which candidate can we work with theory." Peter denied Christ three times, and Jesus still voted him in as head of His church. Paul persecuted Christians and was chosen by God to be a disciple! Voting is an awesome right and a privilege, and we need to exercise that right with great caution and after much prayer.

E   **Be a good example to each other and evangelize others!**—Everything we do makes some kind of a statement. If we help someone, it makes a statement that we care about that person. If we gossip about someone, it makes a statement that we don't care about him or her, even if that wasn't our intent. With and through God's grace, we can set an example for others that will affect their behavior in a positive way. Parents need to set the moral tone in a family, and they can best do this by being the primary educators of their children and by living what they preach. Grace will help them do this. A parent can't use vulgar language and then condemn a son or daughter for doing the same. A parent can't tell a child to live a chaste life if the parent isn't doing so. Pornography, infidelity, immodesty, drunkenness, and unkindness practiced by a parent will set an example for children. Children will forgive parents their mistakes, but children hate hypocrisy, and hypocrisy is teaching children to tell the truth while the parent lives a lie.

Evangelization has to do with proclaiming our faith in God. Some people think that evangelizing is being pushy and self-righteous. Jesus evangelized all over the place during His three years of public ministry, and He is calling us to do the same during our public and private ministry. Calling people to holiness is what evangelization is all about! As a Catholic, I want others to know the truths and treasures of the Catholic faith, and I want to share with everyone my love for the Eucharist. If someone is so moved by my evangelizing that he or she seeks to become a Catholic, then it is God's grace that moved them! I simply allowed myself to be a grace vessel!

And there you have it . . . the formula for chastity! Grace is like the key to the car's ignition—it turns on the motor. Grace turns on our spiritual life and helps keep us on the road to heaven!

I also call this chapter a "rap" up and that's how I'll end, by inflicting on you my corny raps! But first, let me thank you for reading this book. I hope by now that you can easily see that it was written with a little fear, a lot of trepidation, a fair share of humility, and a tremendous amount of love. God loved me so much that He called me out of darkness and asked me to be a light to His precious teens and to all those to whom I speak, and He asked me to be a three-way bulb! It's kind of like the difference between a 40 watt bulb, a 60 watt bulb, and a 100 watt bulb. The 40 watt Christian just *believes*. The 60 watt Christian *believes* and *witnesses* the truth. The 100 watt Christian *believes*, *witnesses*, and *evangelizes*. One of my favorite hymns is "Shine Jesus Shine," and how blessed we are that God is the source of our light and that our light will never grow dim or burn out if we are 100 watt Christians!

Here's my rap for public school teens.

> Chastity is a lifestyle that will keep you on the go.
>
> Happy, healthy, wholesome, and it's not just saying no!
>
> It's a choice . . . a decision . . . a healthy way to live.
>
> If you save sex for marriage, self-respect you'll get and give!
>
> The "safe sex" message is a lie, its argument has holes.
>
> We have to challenge people to pursue much higher goals.
>
> We don't need pills and condoms to keep ourselves intact.
>
> We need to practice chastity, and that's a healthy fact!

Now here's my rap for Catholic and Christian school teens.

Chastity is a lifestyle that will keep you on the go.

Happy, healthy, holy, and it's not just saying no!

It's a value and a virtue, and a Godly way to live.

If you save sex for marriage, self-respect you'll get and give.

The "safe sex" message is a lie, its argument has holes.

We have to challenge people to pursue much higher goals.

We don't need pills and condoms to keep ourselves intact.

We need to honor God's commands and that's a healthy fact!

Which one of these raps do you think I like better? Both of them are corny, and both tell the truth, but only one tells the source of that truth, and that is the one with God in it. God is in both raps, but it is a bum rap that His name may not be mentioned in my public school presentation. Pray that we will be successful in getting Him reenrolled in public schools!

I started out my book talking about Dickens' *A Christmas Carol*, so let me finish it with a quotation from one of the most beloved characters in that story and say to you what Tiny Tim said while perched on his dad's shoulders,

GOD BLESS YOU EVERYONE!

(and if you think Bob Crachit had strong shoulders, try out your Heavenly Father's!!!)

From an Eleventh-Grade Boy:

Dear Molly Kelly,

. . . You treated us like we were mature, responsible, people rather than like morons the way some people treat us. And I thank you for that. I think you have a good message to give to kids and you do it in a good way! The reason I say this is I wholeheartedly agree with you. I respect you because you gave me respect too!! And I'm now aware of all my options as a teenager!!

From a Girl in Middle School:

Dear Mrs. Kelly,

A lot of people at our school talk about sex and want to have sex. I definitely don't want to until I'm married because that is something that is very special in my life and I want it to mean something. My boyfriend wants me to, but I tell him NO, of course. He hasn't asked me anymore since you've come and talked. So I really, really, really appreciate it and thanks once again.

From a Junior:

Dear Molly,

Hi. I just wanted to let you know how much I truly appreciated you coming to our school. I am one of the people that gets in trouble a little more than others. I have had many opportunities to have sex and I'm glad that I haven't done it yet. My feelings about sex before you talked here at my school were like, "well why not?" but not anymore. I don't want to have sex now and I am going to hold off till I'm married. Thank you so much.

FROM A FRESHMAN:

Dear Molly Kelly,

I enjoyed the message you spread in our school today. It actually made teens feel good. My boyfriend and I have had sex and today I decided to "start saving my body again."

FROM A SEVENTH-GRADE GIRL:

. . . I'm only in the 7th grade. But I already had a friend who had sex with her boyfriend. She regretted dearly. I helped her the best I could through her emotional needs. She is very confused, but she is coming out of it. I never thought that I would come in such close contact with things like this. You helped my eyes to be opened. Yes, I would like to date, but I could never think of a boy in "that way." The world is scary, but God will be my light so I know which path I will take.

FROM A FEMALE STUDENT:

. . . I've been thinking a lot about what you said and I have made some decisions about things. You helped me realize that sex isn't everything in a relationship. I have a lot of friends that have had babies and that are pregnant right now. I wish that they could have got advice about things you talked about before they got pregnant.

From Anther Female Student:

Dear Mrs. Kelly,

I was moved by your speech. I didn't think anyone from your generation could look at us in that way. It really was nice of you to talk with us about choices and sex. I had a friend ask me, not too long ago, how far should she let her boyfriend go with her. My only response was not to let him go anywhere.

ADDITIONAL PUBLICATIONS BY MOLLY KELLY

BOOKS

Let's Talk to Teens about Chastity, Public School Version
Let's Talk to Teens about Chastity, Catholic Version
Let's Talk to Teens about Chastity, Spanish Version

VIDEOS

Teens and Chastity, Public School Program, Older Adolescents
Teens and Chastity, Public School Program, Young Adolescents
Teens and Chastity, Catholic Program
Teens and Chastity, Christian Program
Teens and Chastity, Molly Kelly Speaks to Adults
Face to Face with Teens
Abortion Issues

BOOKLETS

Chastity: The Only Choice
Abortion: Beyond Personal Choice

All of the above resources are available through The Center for Learning. For a free catalog containing order and price information and a descriptive listing of titles, contact

> **The Center for Learning**
> Shipping/Business Office
> P. O. Box 910
> Villa Maria, PA 16155
> (800) 767-9090 • FAX (888) 767-8080
> **E-mail:** cfl@stratos.net
> **Web:** http://www.centerforlearning.org/religion.htm

Check the Center's Web site for Molly's speaking schedule, or write to her at the above address.